The Cakebread Cellars
Napa Valley Cookbook

WINE AND RECIPES TO CELEBRATE
EVERY SEASON'S HARVEST

Dolores and Jack Cakebread

with resident chef Brian Streeter

Photographs by Maren Caruso

TEN SPEED PRESS
Berkeley | Toronto

Dedication
With much appreciation to our three sons,
Steven, Dennis, and Bruce, for their help, support, and professionalism
in helping to make our dream come true
and continuing to help it grow for another thirty years.

Ten Speed Press
Box 7123
Berkeley, California 94707
www.tenspeed.com

Distributed in Australia by Simon & Schuster Australia,
in Canada by Ten Speed Press Canada, in New Zealand by
Southern Publishers Group, in South Africa by Real Books,
and in the United Kingdom and Europe by Airlift Book
Company.

Cover and text design by Nancy Austin
Food and location photography by Maren Caruso
Food styling by Kim Konecny and Erin Quon
Photo asistance by Faiza Ali
Photographs on pages 4, 6, and 8 by Jack Cakebread
Photographs on pages 10, 16 (top), 18–19, 20–21,
and 22 by Terrence McCarthy

Library of Congress Cataloging-in-Publication Data

Cakebread, Dolores.
  The Cakebread Cellars Napa Valley cookbook : wine and
recipes to celebrate every season's harvest / Dolores and Jack
Cakebread ; with resident chef Brian Streeter.
    p. cm.
  ISBN 1-58008-508-3
  1. Cookery, American—California style. 2. Cakebread Cellars.
3. Wine and wine making—California—Napa Valley. I. Cakebread, Jack. II. Streeter, Brian. III. Title.
  TX715.2.C34 C33 2003
  641.59794—dc21
                                              2003007728

Printed in China
First printing, 2003
2 3 4 5 6 7 8 9 10 — 08 07 06 05 04

CONTENTS

Sandwiches, Pizzas, & Bread

Pasta & Rice

Seafood & Shellfish

Meat & Poultry

Vegetables & Side Dishes

Desserts

Appendices

ACKNOWLEDGMENTS

Jack and I wish to thank all of our family and our extended family for their friendship, dedication, and professionalism in helping us grow the winery to what it has become over the past thirty years.

We owe a debt of gratitude to Lori Lyn Narlock for not only putting this book into written form but for tasting all of the recipes.

We are delighted that Lisa Ekus, our agent, found our book a home with Ten Speed Press. We've been so lucky to work with all the wonderful people there, especially our editor Julie Bennett and art director Nancy Austin. We also want to express our gratitude to Maren Caruso, who took such lovely photographs.

The Napa Valley College Potters Guild has been very gracious in making the beautiful plates that were used in many of the photos, and for that we thank them.

We are very fortunate to have a great staff, many of whom took time to test the recipes in our book. We want to thank Marny Birkitt, Sylvia Johnson, Connie Gore, Joe Martinez, Mike Barno, Nicole Freitas, Jack Cummings, Nan Brenzel, Nancy DeMerritt, Keith Garlough, Pat Kincaid, Kathy Baldwin, Stephanie Finn, Karen Gary, George Knopp, and Sharon Chew.

We also want to acknowledge Terrance McCarthy, who has captured our winery, friends, and special events with his camera for many years.

And from me, a big thank you to my husband, Jack, for his persistence in encouraging me to record our stories and recipes on paper.

—Dolores

PART I
Cakebread Cellars

INTRODUCTION

The Best Is Yet to Come

HELLO. I'M JACK CAKEBREAD. My wife, Dolores, and I own and operate Cakebread Cellars, a family winery in the Napa Valley. Two of our three sons, Dennis and Bruce, work with us, and our oldest son, Steve, is a valuable consultant for the winery. Dolores and I have been married for more than fifty years. For thirty of those years, we've had the pleasure of transforming Cakebread Cellars from a vision into one of the most respected wineries in California, where we welcome guests from around the globe every day.

Dolores and I like to say that at Cakebread Cellars there aren't any strangers, just friends we have yet to meet. Meeting people, sharing our wines, and gathering for a meal with new and old friends is what has always been the most pleasurable part of our lives and our business.

In our minds the winery and the kitchen aren't any different, the winery is just bigger. Because of that, we treat the two the same. We don't put wine on a pedestal and we don't make art on the plate for the sake of art—we put wine and food on the table to be enjoyed, along with the most important part of any good meal: the company around the table.

As a winery and as a family, we grow grapes, we make wine, we nurture a garden, we cook with the food we grow, and we count our blessings. This is what we do and we love it.

Above: Original winery house, circa 1975. Below: Sturdivant Ranch, 1973.

This Is How We Got Started

FROM THE VERY BEGINNING, Cakebread Cellars has been a labor of love. When we bought the place in 1973 it was a cow pasture with a century-old house that didn't even have a foundation. There wasn't a winery, just an old barn with a dirt floor and walls that leaned this way or that way depending on which direction the wind was blowing.

The ranch then belonged to longtime friends of my family Jack and Helen Sturdivant. The Sturdivants had been living in the Napa Valley, raising cattle, tending walnut orchards, and growing several obscure grape varietals for more than fifty years. In 1973, I stopped by to say hello. It was a visit that would change our lives.

IT BEGAN WITH A CAMERA

I had been building up a reputation as a fine-arts photographer with gallery and museum shows and was also shooting NFL games when I was asked to shoot some photographs of the wine country for Nathan Chroman's book *The Treasury of American Wines*. One miserably cold, gray, and rainy day, I was in Napa Valley to take some photos. It was not a good day for taking photographs, so I decided to get out of the rain by paying a visit to the Sturdivants. It was an uneventful visit, until it came time to leave. I impulsively mentioned that if they ever decided to sell the place, I'd like to buy it. By the time I got home to Oakland that afternoon, they had called and offered to sell it to us.

Buying the Sturdivant Ranch made sense for us for several reasons. Dolores and I had been coming up to Napa pretty regularly and had fallen in love with the area. We were both in our early forties and wanted to do something new that would be a part of our future. At the time, we owned an auto repair shop in Oakland—Cakebread's Garage—which I had purchased from my mother after my father's death. For nearly my entire life I had divided my time between the garage and working on my father's ranch in Contra Costa County. The Napa property would take its place in our lives.

The day after I made the offer to the Sturdivants, Dolores and I drove up to Napa. I was beginning to think it was a futile trip; we didn't really have the means to purchase the ranch. When we arrived, I reluctantly told Mr. Sturdivant that all we had was $2,500—the advance payment I had received for shooting the photographs for Chroman's book. Mr. Sturdivant accepted the money as the down payment, we gave them lifetime rights to live in the house, and we became grape growers.

We immediately went to work, planting a vineyard with the intention of selling grapes to vintners. Within a year, we took a look at our winemaker neighbors and realized we could be doing that too! We took some winemaking classes at the University of California at Davis and absorbed as much information as we could from the people around us—Bob Mondavi, André Tchelistcheff, Louis Martini. We worked around the clock, spending the day in the garage and then making the two-hour roundtrip to Napa afterward to work at the ranch. We spent every weekend up here, too. During the summer I'd work outside doing whatever was needed, from weeding to planting, and then I'd go inside when it got dark and work in the winery for a couple of hours. Dolores took care of the paperwork (and there's a lot of it, as anyone in this business will tell you). We kept that schedule for nineteen years, until we finally sold the garage.

In those early days there was always a shortage of money; everything we had went into the place. Any income we earned was reinvested in the business. We'd sell some wine and then turn around and pay a light bill, buy more grapes, plant more vineyards. We made a barrel, sold a barrel, made two barrels, sold two barrels.

Once we made the wine, the next step was to sell it. I only had weekends available, so during the week I'd go to the public library, pick a city, look up restaurant reviews in the local newspapers, and make a reservation. Then, come Friday night, I'd pack a few bottles, board a red-eye flight, and head for that restaurant.

Dining alone with three bottles of wine on the table always caught the attention of the staff. Invariably, someone would sit down and talk to me. After they tasted the wine they'd ask to buy some; I'd ask them for the name of the best distributor in town; and then I'd call them first thing Monday morning. I'd have to spell my name fourteen times, but slowly I made inroads, and most of those original distributors are still selling our wine today.

Cakebread (the name has been traced back to eleventh-century England, where my father's family were bakers of cakes and breads, tombstone makers, and plush weavers for kings and queens) is now one of the most recognized winery names in the country. Our wines appear on the wine lists of fine restaurants and the shelves of fine wine shops around the world.

Dolores, too, played an important role in building our sales. For the first few years she was our Bay Area

Jack's 1967 El Camino

delivery person. She'd pack up our family station wagon with wine and make the rounds. This was before people really knew our wines and most hadn't even tasted them yet. The first time Dolores made a delivery, the fellow behind the counter in the wine shop pointed at the corner and told her to put the wine there. After that she changed her strategy—and her wardrobe. From then on she wore high heels and a flippy skirt. She never unloaded another case of wine.

At the same time, Dolores was also running the garage. We had two six-button phones installed. One phone was for winery sales and the other was for the shop. Dolores would answer both phones between helping the garage customers while I ran back and forth between Napa and Oakland. It was a frantic pace.

And it's all been worth it. This life is truly special. Our vision, good people, and fortunate circumstances have helped us grow from 157 cases to an annual production of 85,000 cases. It's been a marvelous ride that shows infinite possibilities for the future.

A FAMILY STORY

Cakebread Cellars is a family business. That's what has made us successful. As a family, we own and operate this business on a day-to-day basis. You'll always find a Cakebread on the property—making our wine, running our business, greeting our visitors, and hosting lunches and dinners.

Dolores is the only partner I've ever had. We could not have run and grown this business without each other. Because of her, I could be in two places at once.

Love, fate, call it what you will, we're a lucky pair who have been happily married for more than fifty years. We met in high school in Oakland when Dolores was fourteen years old and I was fifteen. Her family had moved to California from Minnesota five years before. It was wartime, and her mother was a "Rosie the Riveter." Her father was a painter.

My father owned the auto garage and ranch. We grew everything at the ranch—fruits and vegetables, and we had chickens for fresh eggs. During the war these

Dolores in her vegetable garden

items weren't easy to come by, so we'd bring them in to the shop and give them to our customers.

I grew up going back and forth between the ranch and the shop, a habit that held me in good stead when we later ran both the garage and the winery. During high school, Dolores and I worked together along with my mother harvesting almonds and peaches. After high school I earned a scholarship playing football in Santa Rosa. When Dolores graduated, she went to Berkeley and I transferred down there.

Two years later, the Korean War started and I enlisted in the Air Force. I didn't want to leave Dolores before we were married, so she and I and my sister and her beau drove up to Reno the next weekend and had a double wedding. A few weeks later I took Dolores on our honeymoon—a camping trip, her first.

I went off to basic training and was later stationed in Tampa, Florida. Dolores was pregnant with Steve and wanted me to be with her when the baby came along, so she packed up and got on an airplane—in those days it was a propeller-driven machine that made it a very long, slow trip. When she stepped off the airplane, it was 100 degrees with 108 percent humidity. It was miserable.

No one we knew in the Air Force had any extra cash. My pay was only fifty-two dollars a month, so there wasn't a lot to spend on anything but the necessities. When Steve was born the three of us lived in an old apartment building with other service families. We had to save our money just to go to the drive-in movies, where for a buck and a half we could get in and buy a root beer and a hot dog each.

I spent a lot of time in the air during those days, flying around the states and serving in Europe—mostly in England—and in North Africa. When Dennis was due, I went home. Dolores picked me up at the base and here was this little kid, Steve, standing in the back seat. I barely recognized him and he hadn't seen me in so long he didn't know who I was. He started crying and didn't stop for what seemed like days.

When I left for overseas again, my mother gave me a small camera to take pictures for everyone in the family to see where I had been. I was getting on the plane, loaded down with a duffel bag, a rifle, and all this other

Aerial view showing construction of the David Greth Building (aka, "the pond building") with Highway 29 on the left, 1974.

stuff and the camera strap got caught and the camera busted before I could use it. I went to the PX when I got to England and bought a new camera, and that was the beginning of a hobby, part-time career, and the bridge to many new adventures.

From Tampa we moved to Savannah and the government extended my tour—thank you very much! I was discharged a year later and we packed up the kids and came home. Like many people of our generation, we bought my parents' home in Oakland, and they moved to a new place.

We were happy to be back in the Bay Area. Bruce was born shortly after we moved home, which meant Dolores had her hands full with all three boys as I went back to work at the garage with my dad. I also revived the ranch, which my dad had been leasing out for the five years I was in the service.

We began to get settled down in that small house. We bought our first television set, planted a garden, and built a small darkroom in the basement. That year, for Christmas, Dolores gave me a photography workshop session with Ansel Adams as a gift. She claimed to do it for herself because it gave the whole family the chance to take a vacation in Yosemite for two weeks! That was 1957.

Ansel was a workaholic. Our day would start before dawn and go until about ten o'clock at night. Three years later and again in 1966, I went back to study with him. We traveled all over the valley taking shots, printing them, and critiquing them. I learned a lot each time and Dolores and the boys had a ball swimming, fishing, and camping while I was in the workshop.

By my third study with Ansel, I was working full-time at the garage, taking photos on the side, and we had moved to Laguna Avenue in Oakland. It was the first home that we built from the ground up. We spent all of our money on square footage and when we moved in we couldn't afford to fill it. We used some boxes as a shelf for our hi-fi and a card table for our dinner table until we finally could afford to buy some furniture, but even then there wasn't any carpet, just plywood. Eventually we put in carpets, drapes, and furniture.

One luxury we afforded ourselves after furnishing the house was a swimming pool. None of the boys

Jack Cakebread

wanted to mow the lawn, and I sure didn't, so we decided on a pool. It was one of the best things we ever did. Kids from all over the neighborhood would come over and play in it. Years later, one of the kids dropped by the winery and left a note thanking us for the fun he had had in the pool.

We used the pool as incentive for getting the boys to do their chores. They weren't allowed to swim unless Dolores or I were there to supervise and we wouldn't play lifeguard until all the work was done, so they'd help us to get out there quicker. Also, because the rule was that if they fought they'd have to get out of the pool, they made a real effort to always get along.

I think that lesson has stuck with them and has helped them work together here at the winery. In fact, when it was time to pick a chief operating officer, we stepped back and let the boys decide among themselves. Steve and Dennis selected Bruce, but they all play equally important roles in this business.

Steve is a chief financial officer in the software industry and his high-tech perspective, financial advice, and contributions as a winery ambassador all over the world have been invaluable. Dennis, our second son, joined the winery after a ten-year career in banking. He plays an integral role in our business as senior vice president of marketing and sales. Dennis travels around the country to meet with distributors, restaurateurs, and media. He spends much of his time hosting consumer events, such as winemaker dinners.

Our youngest son, Bruce, came here right after graduating from the University of California at Davis and has been here ever since. He left for college when the winery was just a few years old to pursue a degree in pomology—the study of fruits and nuts. When he came home, laundry in tow, he would work with us at the winery on weekends and during the summer. He fell in love with it and transferred from Cal Poly in San Luis Obispo to UC Davis, where he earned a degree in viticulture and enology. In 1978, he joined the winery and two years later he began to assume the winemaking responsibilities at my side. Today he works closely with our winemaker, Julianne Laks, overseeing the production of every bottle of Cakebread Cellars wine.

Besides our sons' labors, we've benefited from the hard work of their wives as well. Sara, Dennis's wife, was an integral part of our public relations efforts until recently when she left to focus on her writing, including the newspaper column she writes for our local paper. Rosemary, Bruce's wife, worked with him in production and winemaking for many years and is now a winemaker at another winery in the valley.

Karen, Steve's wife, has been here for over a decade working with Dolores to make our hospitality team one

From left to right: Bruce, Dolores, Jack, and Dennis Cakebread

of the best in the valley. She travels internationally, assisting me and complementing Dennis's domestic efforts. We've created a great team and we have a pretty good time making it all work.

After going back and forth between the winery and Oakland for nineteen years, Dolores and I sold the garage in 1989. We stayed in Oakland for three more years because both of our mothers were getting up there in age and both still lived independently, so we didn't want to be too far away from them. Ironically, after Dolores's mother told us she was going to live to ninety-six and that we should move, my mother told me she was relieved that we wouldn't be commuting anymore. In 1992 we moved to Napa Valley. Before that, Dolores would always tell people that we slept in Oakland and we lived in Napa. It sure feels good to do both here in the heart of Napa Valley.

GROWING OUR BUSINESS

When we started out, we were so excited about the property that when people phoned to make an appointment to visit the winery we would invite them to tour the property so we could share our dreams and our vision.

The valley was totally different then. Our vineyards were still new and small enough that you could see the highway. There were so few cars on the roads that when a car would pull into our driveway the neighbors would call to see what was going on. It was so casual that often when someone came for a visit they'd find Dolores and me out working in the front yard and think we were property caretakers.

We began working on the land first. The same people who gave us guidance when we decided to make wine were also instrumental in our decision to plant our first vineyard with sauvignon blanc grapes. Most folks were planting cabernet sauvignon and chardonnay, but we were advised to plant sauvignon blanc, and we did. We planted twenty acres of it. Today the same varietal is growing in the same location, right next to the winery house. Of course, it's all been replanted and there's more of it. We also grow cabernet sauvignon and merlot on the same ranch.

Karen Cakebread

When we bought the property it was mostly open pasture. There was on old dirt-floor cow barn on the property, which we used the first year to store tractors and other equipment. We immediately built a twenty-five-square-foot building next to the pond we used for irrigation so we had a place to store the chardonnay we made that year. Three years later that building was expanded and we put fermentation tanks in it, making it our first indoor winery. Today we use that building for meetings and special events. Although it is often referred to as "the pond building" because of its location, it is officially the David Greth Building, in honor of the contractor who built the addition as well as our home and all of our other winery buildings.

In 1980, architect William Turnbull designed our first winery building, the Rutherford building. Initially, we were just going to put a roof over some tanks, but then, in

Rutherford white wine barrel room

the name of energy conservation, we put up walls and insulated it completely. Fourteen years later we tripled the size, and the next year we added the space now used for our offices, where the original barn once stood. In 2000, we built our Oakville building, which we use solely for producing red wines. This allows us to devote the Rutherford building entirely to white wine production.

When the Sturdivants passed on in 1986 we renovated the house. Dolores planted flowers around the house and along the side of the road. Dolores's gardens are gorgeous, part of what makes our winery so magical.

We've taken great strides to build a winery whose architecture is designed to fit into the landscape. The result is an environment that is welcoming and comfortable for the visitors that stop here each day.

When people come to the visitor's center without a tour, we think they're cheated because they don't get to see the pecan trees, the flowers in the courtyard, and the majestic interior of the winery. So when we go home we always make a point to stop in the visitor's center and chat with our guests. We like to remind them that we have full tours available by appointment because we want to share the winery with everyone.

We've Come a Long Way

We've been lucky to meet so many wonderful people from around the world and to have a loyal group of repeat customers. One man was such an enthusiast, he showed up in Napa with his private plane and told us, "I can't get enough of your wine in Texas so I brought my jet and I intend to fill it up with Cakebread Cellars!"

We've come a long way from our early sales. When we made our first chardonnay I went to see Phillip Faight at Groezingers, a retailer in Yountville. I told him, "I have some wine I'd like you to taste." Phillip said,

"Where is it?" "It's still in the barrel," I told him, and I invited him up for dinner.

We still lived in Oakland and didn't have a kitchen at the winery—at that time we barely had a winery—but we did have that first small building next to the pond where we kept a grill and a microwave and we'd cook something up and eat outside. Phillip ate with us that night and tasted our wine for the first time. He then asked to buy all 157 cases. Dolores told him he couldn't buy it all—it was like selling our children! We were very attached to those first vintages.

Phillip was a great customer and our wine sales to him gradually grew. As his customers became our customers, we began to receive requests from them for a

Rutherford building

The original David Greth Building entrance

tour of the winery. We'd tell them, "We don't have a tour, but bring your old clothes and work shoes and we'll find you something to do when you come by."

They'd arrive early Saturday morning and we'd put them to work in the vineyards and around the winery. Dolores would bring up hampers packed with food she'd cooked at home in Oakland and a meal would be their reward for a hard day's work. She'd cook enough for twenty. When the group was bigger, we'd have less to eat and more to drink. No one seemed to notice, since they were always having such a good time.

As this was happening, our following grew, and soon weekends were a bustle of activity. More folks would show up to work, and we'd feed them all. Phillip Faight became our first employee. When he arrived he took a look around and said, "You can't wine and dine the whole world." We could, we did, and we still are today.

We've never advertised—we've grown by word of mouth, which is the best endorsement possible. We don't even have a big sign out front, just the mailbox, and Dolores's flowers. We hope that the next time you spot our colorful blossoms, you'll pull in and raise your glass with us.

—Jack

Our Culinary Adventures

✦

GROWING GRAPES and making fine wine was our only intention when Jack and I purchased the property for the winery in 1973. But preparing delicious food very quickly became equally important to us because we were hosting informal meals every weekend for friends who came by to help out. Before long we were planning our first formal entertaining venture, lunch for our distributor in Reno, who was bringing his troops down for a look around. At the last minute, a couple visiting from Los Angeles got thrown into the mix. We were a little nervous, wondering how it would turn out. We fed them a savory cassoulet and a salad made from produce out of my garden. The lunch lasted more than four hours and everyone had a great time. From that day on, hospitality became the benchmark of our business.

That year, 1975, we also hosted our first open house. One hundred and twenty-five people came to the winery to taste our wines and observe the festivities. We held the open house on a small deck outside of the David Greth Building. To our surprise, and that of our guests, a flock of Canadian geese landed on the pond in the middle of the event to help us celebrate.

Our open house is an annual event. After nearly three decades, one still remains the most memorable for me. We wanted to serve our zinfandel, and we discovered that it was really delicious with freshly made peanut butter that we bought at the Food Mill in Oakland. We decided to serve fresh whole-grain bread that we toasted and spread with the peanut butter. It was a great Saturday afternoon snack and the perfect complement to our zinfandel—a big, hearty wine.

The pairing was quite a hit. A few weeks later we went to dinner at Narsai David's restaurant in Kensington, near Berkeley, California. Narsai was our first restaurant customer and we often went to his restaurant on Monday nights, which was his ethnic cuisine night. On this particular Monday, the waiter—a tuxedo-clad fellow—emerged from the kitchen carrying a tray covered with a white napkin. When he got to our table, he pulled away the napkin with a flourish and revealed a

Cakebread Cellars
Napa Valley Sauvignon Blanc

Our sauvignon blanc grapes are grown primarily on our Winery Ranch and River Ranch properties. These grapes exhibit ripe grapefruit and melon flavors and have a nice amount of acid.

The style of our sauvignon blanc is indicative of traditional French wines made with the sauvignon blanc grape. It exhibits aromas that suggest melon, pear, grapefruit, and lemon, and there are citrus and melon flavors on the palate. It is crisp and has a lingering fruity finish.

My first experience with produce was in high school, when I would help Jack during the almond harvest at his family's ranch. In addition to the almonds, his family also had a small orchard of peaches, apricots, and figs, and Jack's mom had a wartime victory garden where she grew vegetables and raised chickens.

Until Jack enlisted in the Air Force he worked for his father on the ranch every weekend. When we got married I began to help his mother there. She and I would harvest the crops and clean the chickens. Sometimes we'd clean as many as fifty chickens in a single day.

All of the practical knowledge I accumulated working on the ranch put me in good stead when I

Narsai David

Dolores's vegetable garden

five-pound jar of peanut butter, compliments of Narsai. We still laugh about that.

Over time, as more guests joined us for meals, I decided I wanted them to enjoy the food we prepared and to feel good when they left the table. Our meals were light, fresh, and, overall, quite healthy. Herbs and citrus juice were used for greater flavor, olive oil replaced butter, and spices enhanced the richness of the dishes. Not only did people feel great when lunch or dinner was over, but this type of cuisine is also incredibly wine friendly.

THE GARDENS

The same rich soil that we are blessed with for growing grapes is also the source for my pride and joy, my gardens. From the flowers out front that first greet our visitors to the olive trees that surround our winery and the abundant fruits and vegetables we cook with each day, our gardens are as important to us as the grapes we use to make our wines.

planted my first garden in Napa Valley. It was a two-and-half-acre plot that stretched from where the house is clear back to where our current garden sits behind the winery building.

That first garden was mainly vegetables. We had a diverse selection of plants and they were all prolific because of the good soil. At the end of every week, everyone in our family—Jack and I, my parents, Jack's sister—would each take a thirty-five-pound lug box filled with vegetables back to Oakland.

At first I canned a lot of the harvest, wanting to preserve all of the fruits and vegetables we were growing. My father would come over to our house and together we'd can tomatoes and applesauce. We'd make pies, freeze lemon juice, and roast tomatoes. My father and I had a lot of fun putting up those foods.

Once I realized that we could grow vegetables year-round we stopped canning and began using only fresh produce in our daily meals. And as I became more familiar with the property, what I planted changed as well. As a stronger emphasis has been placed on exotic varieties of fruits and vegetables and global ingredients, I've had the chance to grow a much larger assortment of plants than I ever could have when I started.

As my garden at the winery evolved, it also paradoxically shrank in size so that the space could be used for vineyards and for the winery building. Today the garden is three-quarters of an acre, but it is filled with such a vast array of fruits and vegetables that there are almost too many to count. We have over seventeen types of tomatoes alone, and every herb imaginable, from rosemary and tarragon to oregano and several varieties of thyme.

One of my favorite plants is the luffa sponge vine. Luffas are a hybrid created from a cucumber and a zucchini. When the vegetable is left hanging on the vine it dries out and turns brown. At that point, we pick them, peel away the skin, shake out the seeds (saving them for the next year), and the luffa sponges are ready for use. I love showing people the luffa sponges because they are so unusual. Many of our guests from the city are astounded to see the garden and the luffa plant is just another dimension of amazement for them.

Cakebread Cellars
Napa Valley Chardonnay

Sixty percent of the grapes that make up our Napa Valley chardonnay are from the Carneros region. This distinctive area, praised for its cool marine climate, is ideal for grapes that benefit from a slow ripening. Because the cool weather allows grapes to stay on the vine longer they develop great, concentrated flavors that hint at green apple and pear. The other grapes we use come from four other distinctive areas, ranging from warm to cool; respectively, they are the Oak Knoll area of Napa Valley, St. Helena, the Russian River Valley, and Anderson Valley.

On the nose, the chardonnay has wonderful green apple, pear, and subtle oak aromas. In the mouth it is silky, with good depth, and balanced fruit and acidity. The finish is generous.

THE LAND OF OLIVES AND HONEY

We are extremely lucky to have a second garden at our River Ranch, a piece of property we purchased in 1982. Adjoining our original vineyards on the southern side, it is a beautiful site situated on the banks of the Napa River and bordered by oak trees and grapevines.

We grow apples, pears, quinces, pomegranates, peaches, figs, and plums, as well as strawberries, squash, and pumpkins at the River Ranch. It's also where our honey is produced.

When I met Spencer Marshall of Marshall Farms—the bee man in the valley—I invited him to put some of his beehives in our orchard. The honeybees feast on the blossoms from all of the fruit trees and then return to their hive to produce the most delicious honey. In the late 1990s we began to bottle our River Ranch honey and we now sell it in our tasting room along with our housemade vinegar and estate olive oil.

Originally, we planted olive trees because of their beauty. Not too long afterward, we began to harvest the olives. Today we produce our own extra virgin olive oil, which we use in everything we cook.

River Ranch beehives

Recently we planted a new olive orchard of frantoio, leccino, and pendolino trees to complement our existing varietals of manzanillo, sevillano, and picholine. Olives are wonderful because they reach their optimum ripeness just as we finish picking our grapes in late autumn. We can then pick the olives and take them to a co-op where they are pressed and the oil is bottled.

People often ask how I select what we grow. I have always liked to experiment, and the soil and climate are so generous that almost everything can be grown here. I would simply plant something that seemed interesting, we'd eat it, and our taste would guide us, forming the basis of our decision to keep it or not.

SHARING THE WEALTH: THE AMERICAN HARVEST WORKSHOP

We always knew that we were very lucky to be able to tailor our diet to the bounty of our gardens, but that most cooks, even professional chefs, didn't have the same opportunities. We wanted to change that.

In 1986, Jack met Bill Shoaf, then beverage director of the Remington Hotel in Dallas, and over a glass of wine, the two quickly fell into conversation about American cuisine and the challenges of bringing together chefs and food purveyors. During that conversation, the vision for the American Harvest Workshop (AHW) was forged.

We decided to create a nonprofit, educational effort to increase the appreciation of wine, viticulture, and the nutritional and aesthetic qualities of American farm products. To support this effort we established an annual event for chefs, farmers, food artisans, and media to interact, with a focus on developing programs that promote and improve the quality, availability, and marketability of American wine and food.

The following August, in the midst of the grape harvest, we held our first workshop. Our guest chefs were Robert del Grande, from Houston; Dean Fearing, also from Houston; Dallas's John Makin; Mark Miller, from Santa Fe; and San Francisco's Bradley Ogden. They were very excited to be here and to be a part of the harvest. I remember walking into the living room of the winery at 3:00 A.M. to round up the troops for night harvesting, only to find Dean Fearing sitting straight up on the sofa, sound asleep. He didn't want to miss the harvest. Now that's dedication.

About two years after the workshop began, our daughter-in-law Karen joined our culinary team. Within a few years she found her niche focusing on the workshop. Today Karen manages the entire event, from

Cakebread Cellars
Napa Valley Cabernet Sauvignon

Our cabernet sauvignon comes primarily from the Oakville-Rutherford appellations with smaller lots from the neighboring Carneros and St. Helena districts. Diverse vineyard sources as well as clonal variations allow us to craft a finished wine of great complexity and structure. Similarly, small additions of merlot and cabernet franc distinguish it from our 100-percent cabernet sauvignon wines.

Our Napa Valley Cabernet Sauvignon has aromas of cedar wood and blackberry fruit. On entry the flavors are full with subtle notes of black licorice, spice, and pepper. The overall texture of this wine is supple and smooth. There are rich and well-integrated flavors of fruit, such as plum, cherry, and berry, balanced by the vanilla of the small French oak barrels used for aging.

Top: AHW chef Rocco DiSpirito. Above: Dried fruit from AHW purveyor Timber Crest Farms

AHW Chefs (from left to right): Rocco DiSpirito, Resident Chef Brian Streeter, Thomas Moran, and Michael Smith

Dolores with Suzanne Reifers of Laura Chenel's Chevre

Richard Wu of Gourmet Mushrooms with Jack and Rocco DiSpirito

planning the small details to selecting the chefs and making all the arrangements for the purveyors, media, and guests who attend each year.

Since the workshop's inception we've had nearly a hundred chefs from all over the country visit the winery. Each year we hold a "farmers' market" in the courtyard where local purveyors offer samples of their cheeses, lamb, sausages, mushrooms, venison, endive, dried fruit, honey, and chocolate for the chefs to try. After a thorough tasting of every ingredient, the chefs create menus from which they prepare exceptional dishes over the course of the next two nights. We are excited to include

At left, (top): Narsai David plating an AHW dinner; (middle): AHW participants tasting wine; (bottom): AHW Chefs (from left to right): Noel Cunningham, Kelly Mills, Brian Streeter, Dolores, Narsai David, Guenter Seeger, and Marcel Desaulniers

Below: AHW winery tour led by Jack

AHW seminar on wine and food sensory evaluation taught by Michael Weiss,
Professor of Wine and Spirits at the Culinary Institute of America.

some of those delicious recipes in this book to give you a taste of the workshop. We think you'll quickly understand its allure.

OUR CHEFS

In 1986 another important development occurred: we began to use the kitchen in the winery house. It seemed like the minute we moved in there we were entertaining more than ever. At the same time, I realized I was missing my own parties because I was always in the kitchen.

I decided that the time had come to expand our team. I hired our first resident chef, Jim May. Jim was a cook from Auberge du Soleil, an acclaimed resort on the eastern side of the Napa Valley. Jim came to us because he wanted to learn more about wine. We put him to work part-time in the kitchen and part-time in the visitor's center.

When Jim left five years later, we hired Brian Streeter, who was then only twenty-two. Brian had just graduated from the New England Culinary Institute and had come to Napa Valley to work as an intern at Domaine Chandon. Our focus had really shifted to healthy cuisine by the time Brian joined us, and although he had been cooking classic French food, he was encouraged to develop the healthy, fresh dishes that are the signature cuisine of Cakebread Cellars today.

Like Jim, Brian worked in the visitor's center part-time. It was his first experience working with the public. The experience paid off, as Brian became more comfortable talking to visitors, and in many ways it was training for the pivotal role he has grown into as a chef and teacher at Cakebread Cellars.

At Cakebread, Brian has had the opportunity to work with visiting chefs. That exposure has helped him to develop his own style utilizing the best products available. Over the years, he has been instrumental in creating relationships for Cakebread Cellars with local purveyors. His respect for what they produce, grow, and sell is demonstrated by how he showcases their products with the same care that he shows our wines.

Our hospitality calendar keeps Brian busy cooking lunches and dinners, developing recipes to pair with our wines, preparing the wonderful fare that we serve during our open house, teaching cooking classes that emphasize wine and food educaction, and acting as our culinary ambassador at a host of special events. He has a keen talent for showcasing seasonal foods in dishes that are extremely wine friendly, as you will discover when you cook the many recipes he has perfected for this book.

Our second resident chef is Richard Haake. Richard carries on the tradition of working part-time in the visi-

Resident chef Brian Streeter visiting with winery guests

tor's center when he isn't in the kitchen. A native of Georgia, who coincidentally also graduated from the New England Culinary Institute, his style of cooking is elegant with a touch of southern flair—a dynamic complement to Brian's earthy Mediterranean-inspired cuisine.

SPREADING THE WORD

In the late seventies there was a culinary renaissance taking place in the valley and many of the wineries began to offer cooking classes for people interested in learning more about wine and food. I loved attending those classes, and when our visitors began to express a stronger interest in learning about what we were doing here, I began to host my own classes.

The garden was the source of my inspiration for those early classes. Organic produce was just being introduced in health food stores and most of it was unappealing. When people came to the winery I was excited to show them what we grew in our gardens. I wanted them to know what truly fresh produce looked like, how it tasted, and how to cook with it. Those first classes featured recipes for vegetable terrines, salsas, fig desserts, and a lot of tomato dishes.

Our classes have evolved during the years to continually entice people with innovative ideas, better cooking techniques, and sensational food. The cooking classes we offer cover a wider range of topics, but each one still showcases the gardens' bounty and the pleasures of wine and food. All of the classes are now led by Brian and Richard, who work closely with Karen to create a dynamic program for our guests. We host a fabulous selection of classes, both demonstration and participation classes, that range in topic from baking pizzas in our wood-burning oven to picking and cooking with olives. Students come for a tour, learn about wine and food pairing, prepare a special meal, and then sit down to enjoy it—always with a glass of wine. Jack and I often have the pleasure of sharing these meals with our guests. We like to joke that our jobs are to hold a glass of wine in one hand and a bite of food in the other.

Life doesn't get any better than this.

—Dolores

A Winery Life

OWNING AND OPERATING a winery is more than a job. It is a lifestyle and a commitment. Our entire livelihood is ultimately dictated by nature's elements—primarily land and weather. It's not a life for the timid or the weak-kneed. It requires a strong spirit, the ability to persevere, and a desire to succeed that is greater than any adversity.

We've always said, "If you love what you do, it isn't work." This love is what has always driven our winemaking team to produce the best wines that they possibly can regardless of the conditions in which they are doing so.

Before we built the buildings we have now, most of our work was done outside regardless of the weather. If rain wasn't beating down on us, it was sun. Even inside, the work is still challenging on many levels. Sometimes, to keep the wine cold during fermentation it's so cold in the cellar that winter coats and hats are required even though it might be 100 degrees outside. Other times, just as our harvest plan is completed Mother Nature steps in and changes everything. Our winemaking team takes this all in stride and it is their dedication and work ethic that makes our business strong.

One of the most hard-working individuals is our winemaker, Julianne Laks, who's been with us since the mid-eighties. After raising her children, she was returning to her career when she met Rosemary, our son Bruce's wife, who in turn introduced her to Bruce. He hired Julianne and immediately their collaboration was effortless and fruitful. Together they further developed the style of wines we produce.

Recently, after nearly two decades of working with us, Julianne assumed full responsibility of winemaker. From tasting wines in the old lab that didn't have a single window to managing two buildings outfitted with state-of-the-art equipment, Julianne has grown with us, and her infinite ability and talent is present in every bottle of our wine.

Cakebread Cellars Napa Valley Syrah

Grown using four clones, all of our syrah fruit comes from the Carneros region, Napa Valley's southernmost appellation. This area is highly regarded for the cool maritime influences of the bay that suit syrah grapes very well.

Our Napa Valley Syrah possesses an inky black color. On the palate, it displays ripe, intense, dark fruit flavors reminiscent of blackberries and black cherries with hints of licorice and dark chocolate. Our syrah has super dark fruit that is nicely balanced by juicy acidity, a subtle hint of toasty oak, and a smooth, dry, lingering finish.

Our Ultimate Objective

Taste is the single most important factor in every decision we make about wine. We strive to make every bottle taste as good as it possibly can. We want it to taste good to us, good to you, and good with food. This principle is fundamental to every decision we make throughout the entire winemaking process—from where the grapes come from to the makeup of a particular blend, from which barrels are used to how long a wine remains in the bottle before being released.

What makes a wine taste good? Balance. All of the components present in the fruit—flavor, tannins, and acidity—and any flavors imparted during winemaking, from the type of yeast to the barrels we use, must be in balance in the finished wine.

How do we achieve wines that taste good? By letting taste guide us. We taste our wines constantly. Julianne and Bruce will taste as many as forty different wines every day, from harvest until they are put in the barrel or tank for aging. They continue to taste these wines, as individual lots, as blends, and as bottled wines, throughout the wine's entire lifetime.

Good Wines Begin in the Vineyard

Geography is the most critical element in producing wine. We select vineyard sites based on the grapes we want to grow so that we can make the wines we want to produce. We evaluate sites based on several factors, including soil type, climate, and sun exposure. Each of these elements can affect the taste of the grapes, so they must be rigorously evaluated and must match our grape-growing objectives.

Once a site is selected we make sure that every detail during planting is matched to the wine we want to make. We pick rootstocks, the actual part of the plant that is underground, that are disease resistant. Clones, the vine that grows from the rootstock above the ground, are selected based on the taste profiles that fit our proprietary style. The spacing of vines and direction of rows is then is designed to produce concentrated flavors in each grape.

After the vines have been planted, we select trellising, the method by which canes are supported, to allow just the right amount of sunlight to reach the grapes based on the site's location. On the western side of Napa Valley, where it stays cooler, we may want to increase the amount of sun exposure to ensure that the grapes reach maturity. In the eastern part of the valley, where the temperatures are often higher and the sun shines longer, grapes need more shade to prevent ripening before the grapes have fully developed flavor.

Trellising is just one technique we employ. Pruning, like trellising, plays an important role in a grape's ripening process. It also helps to control the concentration of flavor. If canes are cut back, the moisture and energy in a vine will be directed to the fruit instead of the foliage.

Cakebread Cellars Benchland Select Cabernet Sauvignon

Our Benchland Select, a 100-percent cabernet sauvignon, is produced with fruit specifically selected from the bench-lands, the gently rolling foothills of the Mayacamas Mountains on the western side of the Napa Valley. The vineyard's eastern exposure offers cooler temperatures that allow the grapes to mature slowly. The resulting wine reflects the exceptional quality of the fruit from two select vineyards in the Napa Valley's western foothills, with most coming from our own Hill Ranch.

Our Benchland Select displays aromas of an intense red fruit character and the spiciness of mocha, cocoa, and nut-meg. The flavors seamlessly echo its aromas, showing a soft, elegant wine that offers plenty of ripe fruit with a lingering balance of vanilla, cedar, and supple, well-integrated tannins.

(are pollinated) will slowly mature during the growing season. They will develop a flavor profile, go through verasion (change color from their original green to purple for red wines and a darker green for white wines) and finally develop just the right amount of sugar that signals they are ready for harvest.

The grapes that we use to make our wine are predominantly grown on our own vineyards, and those that aren't are purchased from growers that we've enjoyed long relationships with. We share the same values with our growers and work in tandem to produce excellent grapes that we are happy to welcome into the winery.

Oakville red wine building

Three other equally important vineyard practices are the use of cover crops, which help to control the vigor of the vine and ultimately the concentration of flavor in each cluster; judiciously applied fertilization to ensure the vine's proper nourishment; and the management and regulation of water given to each vine.

Ultimately, what we want to achieve with all of the variables involved in growing grapes is to be able to get uniform maturity at a low sugar content throughout an entire vineyard. This makes the best wines because the fruit will be flavorful without being too tart from being underripe or too sweet from being overripe. Grapes that fit this profile lead to wines that are balanced, complex, and food friendly.

The task of picking grapes seems a long way off when the grapes begin their reproductive cycle. It begins in spring when the first buds emerge from the newly pruned vines. As the canes gradually unfurl and leaves begin to appear, the grape clusters—tiny bright green bunches—appear in what seems like an instant. Within a few weeks they show dramatic size increases, and flowers poke out from each individual grape. Those that set

In the early morning hours, grapes are carefully hand harvested,
loaded into bins, and transported to the presses.

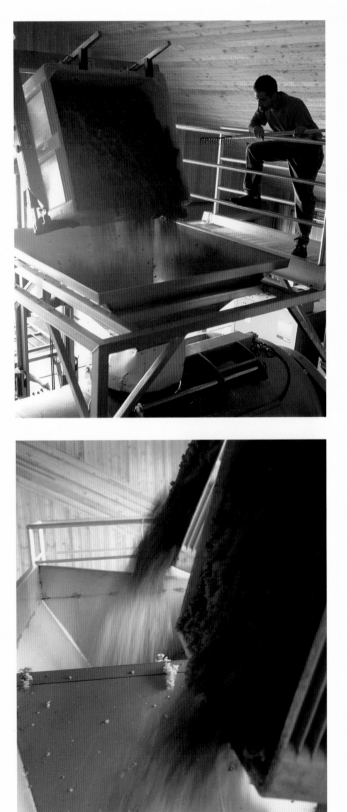

Whole cluster pressing commences under watchful eyes.

Fermentation begins.

INSIDE THE WINERY

We were the first winery in Napa Valley to have separate buildings for red and white wines. Red grapes are sent to our Oakville building and white grapes are shuttled to our Rutherford building. Our location in the center of the valley finds the buildings located on opposite sides of the Oakville-Rutherford border, hence their names.

Having separate buildings for the wines is a luxury that allows us to lavish attention on each without the worry of trying to fit the wines all under one roof. Having two buildings is a little like having two ovens on Thanksgiving. You can cook the turkey in one and all the sides in the other without worrying about having to stop cooking one dish before it's finished because you've run out of oven racks. The same with wine; no wine is ever rushed because we need to make space.

Our grapes are delivered to the winery in half-ton bins to prevent the fruit from being crushed in transport. Our white grapes are whole-cluster pressed and our red grapes are destemmed and gently crushed. The juice is then transferred to tanks and either left to soak overnight or inoculated with yeast to start to the fermentation process.

Cakebread Cellars Vine Hill Ranch Cabernet Sauvignon

Our Vine Hill Ranch Cabernet Sauvignon is a wine born of a longtime partnership with Bob Phillips and his family. The Phillips family has been growing outstanding grapes for us since 1981 on their property that is situated along Oakville's gently sloping western hillsides. Until 1997, the grapes that the Phillipses grew for us were added to our Benchland Select. We decided that the grapes were so special they deserved a single vineyard bottling.

Vine Hill Ranch Cabernet Sauvignon is layered and complex. From the deep, dark colors and the intense aromas of blackberry, plum, vanilla, and cassis to the flavors of dark berries and chocolate, each layer unfolds slowly and deliberately. It has a smooth texture, firm tannins, and a long finish.

Cakebread Cellars Chardonnay Reserve

Ninety percent of the grapes used for our Chardonnay Reserve come from the Carneros region, an area acclaimed for growing some of the best chardonnay grapes in California. The vineyards where we grow our grapes have a reputation for producing outstanding chardonnay wine.

Our Chardonnay Reserve displays aromas of vanilla, melon, and pear. It has a full body, round texture, and hints of minerals, pineapple, and lemon flavors on the palate.

Once fermentation is completed the whites are divided among tanks and small French oak barrels for aging for several months. Our white wines and lighter reds, like our Rubaiyat, are bottled and released within a year, except for our Chardonnay Reserve, which is bottle aged for over one year before release.

Following fermentation of our red wines, most are left to macerate—soak with the skins in the juices for a few weeks to extract color, flavor, and tannins. During this period they are racked and returned, transferred from one barrel to another and back again to soften the tannins through exposure to oxygen. The wines are then put in barrels for eighteen to twenty-six months before being bottled and further aged and then released.

Throughout this process, the wines are constantly tasted. Although we have a general game plan for all of our winemaking, wine is an organic substance and constant monitoring through sensory evaluation is the only measure of when it is ready for the next stage of the winemaking process.

There is a kind of joke among winemakers: if your hands aren't purple and black from the wine, then your tongue better be, or you aren't doing your work. Ask Bruce and Julianne to say "Ah" and you'll know they are doing their job. They are always in the cellar tasting. And each wine they taste is evaluated carefully because the bottom line is the wine must always taste great. All of our experience, all of our knowledge, all of our work is for naught if the wine doesn't taste good.

Oakville winery fermentation room

WINE AND FOOD PAIRING

We strive to make wines that are food friendly, meaning that they have balanced fruit, acid, and tannins. Equally important to us is to produce dry wines. Our objective is to always showcase the work of the winemaker and the chef with equal aplomb. One should never outshine the other.

There are dozens of rules and philosophies surrounding the pairing of a specific wine with a specific dish. While many of these maxims may result in delicious combinations, ultimately the pleasures of consuming wine and food are purely subjective.

This isn't to say that there won't be a consensus among an entire group of people as to the preference for a particular wine paired with a specific dish, but this does not make it true for all people. For example, there are traditional pairings that have stood the test of time, such as goat cheese with sauvignon blanc and filet mignon with cabernet sauvignon. These matches are accepted as a general pairing rule; however, some people love chardonnay with beef, others love merlot with chevre. These are personal preferences that cannot be argued or explained any more than you can rationalize a favorite color or type of music.

At Cakebread Cellars we produce fine wines that we enjoy drinking and we pair them with food that we take pleasure in eating. The choices we make when we pair wine and food are based on different factors. Often a wine is chosen as part of a menu. In that case, when more than one course is served, more than one wine will be selected. We always begin with lighter wines and proceed to wines with greater intensity. For example, we will serve a light, crisp sauvignon blanc with a salad course, a chardonnay with a main course, and one of our more full-bodied red wines, such as a cabernet sauvignon, with a cheese course to end the meal.

Sometimes we select a wine based on our moods or on the season and the dishes that reflect the weather. We may want to drink a refreshing chilled wine, like

Above: Cellar master Brian Lee
Below: Winemaker Julianne Laks

Cakebread Cellars
Napa Valley Merlot

The grapes for our merlot come from Carneros and both the middle and upper Napa Valley. From the southern Carneros region, where cooler temperatures produce fruit with higher acids and true varietal characteristics, we obtain merlot with dark fruit aromas and flavors. In Rutherford, where temperatures are generally much warmer throughout the day, our merlot fruit exhibits bright, forward flavors of red berry and cherry. Combining grapes from these two areas produces wines of extraordinary depth and complexity.

Our Napa Valley Merlot displays a dark purple color with aromas of blackberry and subtle hints of coffee, cedar, nutmeg, and vanilla. On the palate, fresh plum and cherry flavors mix with black pepper, cassis, and a touch of oak. It has a rich, silky texture, complex flavors, and a lengthy finish.

you and hope that you will enjoy the combinations of flavors as much as we do. Our suggestions are the results of tasting and evaluating. By continually familiarizing ourselves with our tastes we are able to determine what we like best. We encourage you to try as many combinations as possible to discover your own favorites or simply drink the wine varietals you like; a wine you love will taste good with any food.

COOKING WITH WINE

We use wine to cook with in a wide variety of dishes. It's used for marinating, deglazing, and braising. It is almost always added before or during the cooking process so that the alcohol is cooked away and doesn't interfere with the flavor of the final dish.

There are two predominant reasons why wine is used in cooking. The first is that it adds an acid compo-

our sauvignon blanc, chardonnay, or Rubaiyat, with a summer salad or our robust, concentrated syrah, cabernet sauvignon, or merlot with a hearty stew on a cold winter night.

While we tested and tasted each of the recipes in this book, we tried many wines at the same time to pick the one we liked the best with each dish. There were usually several of us in the room—at least four and as many as ten. Often, we all selected the same wine as our favorite match with the selected recipe. But it wasn't unusual for us to realize that more than one wine tasted delicious with the dish and on a few occasions we each had a favorite that was different than the next person's.

We've included our wine preferences with each recipe, except for the side dishes and most of the desserts. Wines have not been included for side dishes because the main course should guide your wine decision. Desserts, which are often sweet, can impose an unpleasant taste on dry wine, making it taste more tannic and harsh, so for that reason we prefer not to serve wine with most desserts. There are exceptions, though, as you will discover in this book and in your own experiences.

All this said, we've provided these suggestions for

Cakebread Cellars Pinot Noir

We grow our pinot noir grapes in the cool Carneros and Anderson Valley regions using six clones that result in structures and flavors that complement each other perfectly. They offer an array of characteristics, from round and soft to great complexity and tannin structure, resulting in a wine with great balance.

Our Napa Valley Pinot Noir displays an attractive light red garnet color. On the nose there are ripe fruit aromas that meld with hints of allspice and clove. In the mouth, rich, opulent flavors give way to a lengthy finish.

nent to the dish it is used in, which brings forth the flavors of the other ingredients and adds what is often described as a brightness. The acid can also act as a meat tenderizer, which is why wine is added to marinades and stews when a tougher cut of meat is cooked.

The second reason that wine is used in a dish is that wine acts as a bridge to connect the flavors of that dish to the wine being served. This is a common technique used to help pair a wine with food. Although it isn't imperative that you cook with the same wine you plan to drink, it is a standard practice that only wines suitable for drinking be used for cooking. If a wine doesn't taste good enough to drink it can ruin the taste of a dish that it's added to.

SERVING WINE

We don't stand on ceremony here at the winery. We believe that wine should be enjoyed without any fancy trappings, but there are a few things that can affect the taste of wine. The first is temperature. Wine that is served too cold will mask the flavors of the wine and wine that is too warm will taste flat, emphasizing alcohol and oak flavors.

Wines that are meant to be served chilled should be no cooler than 54°F. Wines intended for room temperature should be no warmer than 59°F. In fact, it is better to chill a red wine slightly than to let it get warm.

But don't get carried away, especially if you want to keep wine cool at the table. The best way to keep wine chilled is to fill an ice bucket with ice, place a kitchen towel over the ice, and place the bottle over the towel.

We often decant old wines to avoid the sediment that accumulates in the bottle and give them a breath of fresh air. We also decant young red wines to soften them with exposure to oxygen.

We are fortunate to have a large inventory of glasses here at the winery and are able to serve each wine varietal in a Riedel glass designed specifically for it. The different shapes of the glasses allow the aroma of the wines to be enjoyed to their fullest potential and direct

the wine to the proper areas in your mouth to make the greatest taste impact. Also, we prefer glasses with thin rims because they feel better, lighter. All that being said, any glass that you like, for any reasons that you like it, will work well because the bottom line is that drinking and enjoying wine is a personal preference.

BRINGING IT ALL TO THE TABLE

What we cook, eat, and drink is heavily influenced by the seasons. You will discover when reading and cooking from this book that our recipes showcase the freshest foods available each season. Each chapter of recipes follows the seasons in the same way that our table does.

It all begins in spring, the season of renewal. When winter recedes and the cold weather begins to dissipate, the vineyards wake up from their sleepy existence and their foliage slowly begins to appear. This magical occur-rence signals that the earth is warming up and life is about to get busier. It is about this time that we embrace the bounty of spring. Asparagus, artichokes, and tender spring lamb all take center stage on our menu, and fresh fruit, like strawberries and rhubarb, are foremost on everyone's mind for dessert.

The time between bud break and harvest, when the first grapes are picked, is known as growing days. During this time the vineyards are transformed into vig-orous, lush rows of green. The gardens burst with an abundance of summer fruits and vegetables, from toma-toes, melons, and corn to peaches, eggplants, and plums. Outdoor cooking and dining become de rigueur for pure pleasure.

As autumn nears, harvest begins and there is no busier time in Napa Valley. The weather changes and consequently the garden yield transitions from warm-weather crops to the signature vegetables of the season—squash, broccoli, and cabbage. These rustic, wholesome ingredients find their way into meals alongside roasted pork, grilled fish, and chicken cooked under a brick, all while the fruit brought into the winery is magically transformed from mere grapes to exquisite nectar.

When the fury of autumn's activities wind down and the cold weather takes root, the table offers a respite with soul-satisfying dishes like braised chicken, stews, and oven-roasted potatoes. Winter menus make great use of herbs and spices to create robust flavors and of long, slow cooking methods that result in rich, complex tastes. During this quiet season, when the vines are dormant, you'll find our menu is filled with hearty, substantial dishes as the reward for a year's worth of work.

Cooking and eating foods at the peak of their season is a pleasure within reach no matter where you live. If you don't have a garden you can seek out locally grown and seasonal foods at farmers' markets and specialty stores. When you live this way everything tastes more wonderful.

Cakebread Cellars Rubaiyat

This very popular wine was named after the famous poem *Rubáiyát,* by tenth-century Persian mathematician, philosopher, and astronomer Omar Khayyám. The constant in Rubaiyat's blend over the years has been food-friendly pinot noir wine, which makes up ninety percent or more of this red wine blend. Additionally, a small amount of syrah is added to bring forward the pinot noir's vibrant raspberry and bright cherrylike flavors. It is a light-bodied red wine blend meant to be served slightly chilled.

Cakebread Cellars Three Sisters Cabernet Sauvignon

This cabernet sauvignon is sourced from the Napa Valley's eastern hillsides, on the cusp of Oakville and Rutherford. The common characteristics of these vineyard sites include a steep terrain of rocky, fire-red volcanic soils, substantial afternoon sunshine, and low rainfall. These elements create the ideal growing conditions for densely flavored fruit.

The aromas of the Three Sisters Cabernet Sauvignon are reminiscent of black fruit and rich vanilla. On the palate the wine is a rich and balanced blend of both red and black fruit characteristics with hints of mocha and vanilla. Overall, this wine has a profound depth, complexity, and an incredibly long finish.

PART II

The Recipes

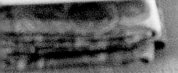

Appetizers

Smoked Salmon Tartare on Belgian Endive

We are lucky to be blessed with the presence of so many great food purveyors in the Napa Valley and surrounding counties. One of the purveyors we rely on is fishmonger Mathew Hudson, who owns a wonderful seafood shop in Napa called Omega 3 Seafoods. Mathew carries a great selection of fresh seasonal fish and smoked fish that he smokes at his shop. At the winery this hors d'oeuvre is made with Mathew's cold-smoked salmon, which has a silky texture. Unlike hot-smoked fish, which has a flaky texture, cold-smoked salmon can be sliced or minced.

SERVES 4 TO 6

4 ounces cold-smoked salmon, minced

1 large shallot, minced

1 tablespoon capers, chopped

1 teaspoon extra virgin olive oil

1/2 teaspoon chopped tarragon leaves

1/4 cup crème fraîche

1 teaspoon fresh lemon juice

1/2 teaspoon minced lemon zest

3 heads Belgian endive

Minced fresh chives, for garnish

Combine the salmon, shallot, capers, olive oil, and tarragon in a small bowl. Set aside.

Put the crème fraîche, lemon juice, and lemon zest in a bowl. Whisk until soft peaks form.

Separate the endive leaves and trim to 3-inch lengths. Arrange the large endive leaves on a flat surface. Reserve the smaller leaves for another use. Spoon about $1/2$ teaspoon of the crème fraîche mixture onto the end of each endive leaf and top with 1 teaspoon of the smoked salmon tartare. Sprinkle with the chives and transfer to a serving dish.

Enjoy with Cakebread Cellars Napa Valley Chardonnay or a chardonnay with balanced fruit and acidity with hints of oak.

SPRING

Artichoke Leaves with Prawns and Aioli

In 1997, I posed for a photograph in *Wine Spectator* magazine holding one of my prized artichokes. From then on people came to think of me as Dolores the Artichoke Lady. Many people are surprised when they learn that the artichoke in the picture came from our garden. Every spring there are lots more like it that are used in recipes such as this one.

SERVES 4 TO 6

ARTICHOKES

2 artichokes, stemmed

1/4 cup white wine vinegar

2 cloves garlic, smashed

2 (1/2-inch-wide) strips lemon zest

2 teaspoons kosher salt

1 bay leaf

PRAWNS

6 cups water

1/3 cup white wine vinegar

3 (1/2-inch-wide) strips lemon zest

2 small dried red chiles

2 bay leaves

1 tablespoon kosher salt

1/2 pound medium prawns, unpeeled, tails on

1 cup aioli (page 210)

Hot paprika, for garnish (Spanish paprika is preferable)

To make the artichokes: Put the artichokes, vinegar, garlic, lemon zest, salt, and bay leaf in a saucepan large enough to hold the artichokes comfortably. Cover with cold water. If a plate will fit in the pot, place the plate on the artichokes to keep them submerged. Bring to a boil over high heat. Decrease the heat to medium and cook at a low simmer for 20 to 30 minutes, depending on size, or until a knife can be easily inserted into the bottom. Remove the plate. Remove from the heat and let sit in the liquid until cool. This will help retain the color.

To make the prawns: Combine the water, vinegar, lemon zest, chiles, bay leaves, and salt in a large saucepan. Bring to a boil over high heat. Add the prawns and remove from the heat. Let sit for 2 to 3 minutes, until the prawns are bright orange and firm. When cool enough to handle, peel, leaving the tails intact. Cut in half lengthwise and devein.

To assemble, remove the outer artichoke leaves that are tender to the bite but firm enough to maintain their shape when picked up. Reserve the palest center leaves (the heart) and bottoms for another use. Spread the leaves on a flat surface and spoon a dollop of the aioli on the tender end. Place a piece of prawn on the aioli and sprinkle with the paprika. Arrange on a decorative plate and serve.

Enjoy with Cakebread Cellars Sauvignon Blanc or a sauvignon blanc that offers a good, crisp, fruity finish and prominent citrus flavors.

SPRING

Crostini with Asparagus and Spring Garlic

Spring garlic, sometimes called green garlic, makes an appearance each spring (before the cloves begin to form), usually at farmers' markets and gourmet markets. We grow our own in the garden, planting the cloves in late fall and harvesting the mature heads when the greens that grow aboveground begin to lie down. Spring garlic looks a little like a fat-bottomed green onion and tastes like a mild version of mature garlic. Because mature garlic is much stronger in flavor it shouldn't be used as a substitute.

SERVES 4 TO 6

24 ($^1/_4$-inch-thick) slices sweet baguette, cut on
    the diagonal

$^1/_2$ cup extra virgin olive oil plus additional for garnish

4 spring garlic bulbs with greens, cut into
    paper-thin slices

16 stalks pencil-thin asparagus, tough ends removed
    and discarded

$^1/_4$ pound Teleme cheese

Freshly ground black pepper

Preheat the oven to 400°.

Brush both sides of the bread slices with $^1/_4$ cup of the olive oil. Spread the slices on a baking sheet and bake for about 7 minutes, until slightly golden. Set on a cooling rack.

Increase the oven temperature to 450°.

Heat the remaining $^1/_4$ cup olive oil in a small saucepan over medium heat. Add the garlic and cook, stirring occasionally to prevent browning, for 5 to 7 minutes, until wilted and soft. Remove from the heat and set aside.

Bring a large high-sided skillet of salted water to a boil over high heat. Add the asparagus and cook for 1 minute, until barely al dente. Drain and submerge in an ice water bath. Cut each stalk into 2-inch lengths to fit on top of the crostini. For a fancier look you can use just the tip of the asparagus, reserving the rest of the spear for another use.

Spoon a small amount of the garlic over each crostini slice. Place 2 pieces of asparagus over the garlic and top with about $^1/_2$ teaspoon of the Teleme (the cheese is very soft and can be easily scooped with a spoon). Bake for about 3 minutes, until the cheese is hot. Sprinkle with pepper and drizzle with extra virgin olive oil. Serve warm.

Enjoy with Cakebread Cellars Sauvignon Blanc or a complex sauvignon blanc with a hint of spice dispersed in the clean fruit flavors.

Spinach Balls with Mustard-Sabayon Sauce

Shortly after Jack and I began entertaining at Cakebread Cellars, I wanted to create a healthy alternative to spanakopita, one of our favorite foods. This was the recipe I devised, which uses Butter Buds, a butter substitute, to reduce the fat. The mustard sauce adds an interesting kick. These spinach balls are still one of our favorites for a little snack to enjoy with a glass of sauvignon blanc.

SERVES 4 TO 6

MUSTARD SAUCE

2 tablespoons white wine vinegar

2 tablespoons dry mustard

$^1/_3$ cup sauvignon blanc or other dry white wine

1 egg

3 tablespoons Dijon mustard

1 teaspoon sugar

Kosher salt

Freshly ground black pepper

SPINACH BALLS

20 ounces (about 3 large bunches) fresh spinach leaves

2 cups herb stuffing mix

2 shallots, minced

4 green onions, minced

$^1/_4$ cup finely grated Parmigiano-Reggiano

Pinch of freshly ground nutmeg

6 tablespoons reconstituted Butter Buds or unsalted butter

2 small eggs, beaten

To make the sauce: Stir together the vinegar and dry mustard to form a paste. Let sit at room temperature for 1 hour.

Whisk together the wine, egg, Dijon mustard, and sugar in a small nonreactive saucepan. Add the dry mustard mixture and heat over low heat, whisking continuously, for 4 to 5 minutes, until the mixture has the consistency of custard. Season to taste with salt and pepper. Cover and refrigerate for at least 4 hours and up to 24 hours for the flavors to soften.

To make the spinach balls: Preheat the oven to 350°. Coat a baking sheet with olive oil.

Rinse the spinach and drain in a colander. (Leave a bit of water clinging to the leaves.) Heat a wide saucepan with high sides over medium-high heat, add the spinach in small batches, and cook, stirring, for 2 to 3 minutes, until wilted. Transfer to a colander to drain and then rinse under cold water to stop the cooking process. Repeat until all of the spinach is cooked.

Squeeze the spinach between your hands to eliminate any liquid, and chop into a fine mixture. Put in a bowl. Crush the herb stuffing mix in a food processor until fine. Add to the spinach. Add the shallots, onions, Parmigiano, and nutmeg and stir to mix well. Add the Butter Buds and eggs and stir to completely incorporate. Shape into walnut-sized balls, about 1 tablespoon each, and place on the prepared baking sheet. Bake for 12 to 15 minutes, until firm. Serve warm with the mustard sauce at room temperature for dipping.

Enjoy with Cakebread Cellars Sauvignon Blanc or a light sauvignon blanc that is enjoyable as an aperitif.

SPRING

Crostini with Beet Tartare and Goat Cheese

Beets taste best when they are freshly plucked from the soil where they are grown. Our garden yields a lovely crop of beets each year that are extremely tasty, and they are even more so when roasted. The trick to making this hors d'oeuvre is to mince the beets very fine so that they can be pressed down into the goat cheese and won't tumble off. Once roasted, beets are easy to peel. You can use your fingers or a clean towel and rub the skins off or you can gently scrape them off with a paring knife. At the winery we make this with an assortment of beets for a striking presentation. If you want to use more than one type of beet, keep them separate or the juices will bleed and the mixture will become one homogenous hue.

SERVES 4 TO 6

4 small chioggia or golden beets

24 ($1/4$-inch-thick) slices sweet baguette, cut on the diagonal

$1/4$ cup extra virgin olive oil

1 heaping tablespoon minced shallots (about 1 small shallot)

2 teaspoons sherry vinegar

2 teaspoons fresh dill, minced

Kosher salt

Freshly ground black pepper

5 ounces fresh goat cheese, at room temperature

1 tablespoon chopped fresh chives

Preheat the oven to 400°.

Trim and discard the greens from the beets. Wrap the beets in aluminum foil and bake for 45 minutes to 1 hour, until tender when pierced with the tip of a knife. Let cool.

While the beets are cooking, brush both sides of the bread with 2 tablespoons of the olive oil. Spread the slices on a baking sheet and bake for about 10 minutes, until crisp and golden brown. Let cool.

Peel the beets by gently rubbing the skin away with your fingers and then cut them into a $1/8$-inch dice or fine mince. Transfer to a bowl. Add the shallot, the remaining 2 tablespoons olive oil, and the vinegar. Stir to mix well. Add the dill and season to taste with salt and pepper.

In a small bowl, mash the goat cheese with the back of a spoon until creamy. Spread 1 teaspoon over each bread slice. Scoop a heaping teaspoon of the beet tartare into the tip of a soup spoon and spread over half of the goat cheese, pressing down to compact the beet tartare against the goat cheese. Sprinkle the center of each crostini with the minced chives.

Enjoy with Cakebread Cellars Sauvignon Blanc or a crisp, versatile sauvignon blanc with a citrus essence.

SPRING

Phyllo Purses Filled with Goat Cheese, Chives, and Lemon Zest

These goat cheese purses are an entertainer's best friend. The purses can be assembled and frozen for up to a week or two before being baked. The best way to make them is to use clarified butter, which is troublesome to make in small batches, so the amount prepared for this recipe will result in leftover butter. It will last for up to three months if it is stored in the refrigerator in an airtight container. During the holidays, substitute dried cranberries and orange zest for the chives and lemon zest.

SERVES 4 TO 6

1 cup (2 sticks) butter

4 ounces fresh goat cheese, at room temperature

2 teaspoons finely chopped chives

$1/2$ teaspoon chopped lemon zest

3 sheets phyllo dough, thawed

Heat the butter in a small saucepan over low heat until melted and it begins to bubble or simmer, about 10 minutes. When it stops bubbling, remove from the heat and skim away any solids that are on top. Use while warm or store for later use.

Combine the cheese, chives, and lemon zest in a bowl. Mash with the back of a spoon until smooth. Set aside.

Unfold the phyllo, remove one sheet, and cover the remaining sheets with a damp kitchen towel. Lay a sheet of phyllo on a flat surface and brush evenly with just enough of the clarified butter to coat it. Arrange a second sheet over the phyllo and brush with butter. Repeat with a third sheet of phyllo. Cut into thirty 2-inch squares. Place a teaspoon of the cheese mixture in the center of each square and pull the edges up to form a purse. Arrange on a baking sheet and place in the freezer for at least 1 hour, until frozen. At this point, the phyllo purses can be transferred to an airtight container and stored in the freezer until ready to use.

When ready to bake, preheat the oven to 400°. Bake for about 10 minutes, until the tips are golden brown. Serve warm.

Enjoy with Cakebread Cellars Sauvignon Blanc or a crisp sauvignon blanc with notes of fresh fruit flavors and that is light on the palate.

SPRING

❧

Pascal Olhats's California Fruits de Mer

In 1993, Pascal Olhats joined a fantastic group of chefs and wine professionals for our workshop. Born and raised in Normandy, France, Pascal earned his American acclaim as the chef of Newport Beach, California's, eponymous Pascal's. Arriving at the workshop with a reputation for specializing in seafood, he quickly went to work demonstrating how he achieved it. This elegant recipe is a good example of Pascal's talent for creating sublime combinations of the sea's treasures. It is very rich, so three to four oysters per person will be sufficient as an appetizer before a meal.

SERVES 4 TO 6

18 fresh oysters

2 tablespoons fresh lemon juice

1 shallot, minced

1/4 cup crème fraîche

1 teaspoon chopped dill

1/4 teaspoon Worcestershire sauce

Freshly ground black pepper

2 ounces smoked salmon, finely diced

Shuck the oysters as described on page 50, reserving all of the oyster liquid and one half of each shell.

Combine the lemon juice and shallot in a bowl. Stir in the liquor from the oysters. Add the crème fraîche and dill and stir until thoroughly combined. Add the Worcestershire and a pinch of pepper.

Spoon a small amount of the crème fraîche mixture over each oyster. Top with even amounts of the smoked salmon and serve on a decorative platter.

Enjoy with Cakebread Cellars Sauvignon Blanc or a crisp, light sauvignon blanc that exhibits lots of citrus characteristics.

❀ SPRING

Spanish-Spiced Pork Brochettes

"A jug of wine, loaf of bread, and thou" is one of the most familiar phrases used to express the pleasures of wine, food, and good company. The line, taken from a poem by tenth-century poet Omar Khayyám, was the inspiration for our Rubaiyat wine, a lighter-style red wine ideal for chilling. These savory grilled pork brochettes were made to be enjoyed with our Rubaiyat because its light, refreshing taste complements the slightly spicy marinade, which is flavored with Spanish paprika, a smokier-tasting paprika than the Hungarian type.

SERVES 4 TO 6

1 pound boneless pork loin, cut into 3/4-inch cubes

2 tablespoons extra virgin olive oil

2 teaspoons dry sherry

2 cloves garlic, minced

1 1/2 teaspoons sweet paprika (Spanish paprika is preferable)

1 teaspoon fresh thyme, chopped

1/2 teaspoon ground cumin

1/2 teaspoon freshly ground black pepper

20 five-inch wooden skewers

Kosher salt

1 lemon, cut into wedges

Light and heat a charcoal grill to high heat 20 to 30 minutes prior to cooking the pork.

Set the pork in a shallow bowl. Combine the olive oil, sherry, garlic, paprika, thyme, cumin, and pepper in a small bowl. Pour over the pork and let sit at room temperature for at least 20 minutes. This can be prepared up to four hours in advance, covered with plastic wrap, and refrigerated.

Soak the skewers in water for 20 minutes. Thread 4 to 5 pieces of pork onto each skewer, bunched together at one end. Set a strip of aluminum foil on the grill. Season the pork with salt and place on the grill with the exposed wood part of the skewers set over the foil to prevent them from burning. Cook for 2 minutes, turning once or twice, until browned on all sides. Arrange on a plate with the lemon wedges and serve. Squeeze the lemon over the skewers before eating.

Enjoy with Cakebread Cellars Rubaiyat or a light red table wine that can be served slightly chilled.

Barbecued Oysters with Chipotle and Lime

Tomales Bay, which is located on the Northern California coast, is home to Hog Island Oysters, an aquafarm that employs the most rigorous of environmentally sound conditions. The result is shellfish absolutely worth eating. Owner and founder Michael Watchorn raises several succulent types of oysters. One of our favorites is the Hog Island Sweetwater, a sweet, plump oyster we enjoy grilling. This recipe is designed for three oysters per person, but they are so popular that you may want to increase the portions to keep up with demand.

SERVES 4 TO 6

18 large oysters, scrubbed and rinsed

$^1/_2$ cup Chipotle-Lime Butter (page 212)

1 lime, cut into wedges, for garnish

To prepare the oysters: The easiest way to shuck an oyster is to fold a thick kitchen towel around the oyster and, holding it tight in your hand, with your other hand, insert a shucking knife into the pointed end, or shell hinge. Twist the knife slightly until you can pop the top shell and unlock the hinge. Slide the knife around the edge to the front and underneath the top shell to cut the oyster muscle attached to the top of the shell. Remove the top shell and slide the knife under the meat of the oyster, cutting around the edge to release it from the shell entirely, making it easier to eat. Don't remove the oyster from the shell.

Twenty minutes before serving, light and heat a charcoal grill to high heat.

Put the oysters on the grill. Cook for 1 to 2 minutes, until the liquid begins to bubble and the oysters begin to curl around the edge. Top each oyster with a small spoonful of the chipotle butter. Transfer to a serving dish. Serve with lime wedges. Squeeze the lime over the oysters before eating.

Enjoy with Cakebread Cellars Sauvignon Blanc or a dry white wine with nuances of citrus in both the aromas and flavors.

SUMMER

Scallop and Green Onion Brochettes with Curry

The pastel colors of the scallops and onions threaded together on the skewers are very attractive, especially when stacked on a plate. Our chef, Brian, likes to arrange the skewers end to end to form a square and then stack them on top of each other in the same pattern until they form a virtual box. It is an unexpected way to present the skewers and very dramatic. Tamari—a dark, wheat-free version of soy sauce—adds a splash of caramelized flavor as well as a touch of color to the scallops. It is easy to find in most grocery stores that sell Asian food products.

SERVES 4 TO 6

16 five-inch wooden skewers

2 bunches (about 12) green onions, washed and
    ends trimmed

16 large (about 1 pound) sea scallops, quartered

1/2 cup grapeseed oil

2 tablespoons curry powder

Dash of low-sodium tamari

Soak the skewers in water for 20 minutes.

Bring a small saucepan of water to a boil over high heat. Cut the green onions into 1-inch pieces beginning at the bottom of the whites until the dark green part is reached. Save the green parts for another use. Drop the white pieces in the water and cook for 30 seconds. Transfer immediately to a colander to drain. Rinse under cold water.

Thread four scallops and three green onion pieces in an alternating pattern onto the skewers. Set in a shallow nonreactive baking dish. Whisk together the oil and curry powder in a small bowl. Pour over the scallops and refrigerate for 2 to 3 hours, turning once or twice.

Heat a large nonstick skillet over high heat. Add the skewers and drizzle some of the curry oil over the scallops. Cook for 1 minute per side, until lightly browned. Add the tamari, shake the pan to distribute the sauce evenly, and remove from the heat. Arrange on a decorative dish and serve.

Enjoy with Cakebread Cellars Napa Valley Chardonnay or a fruity chardonnay with a slight hint of oak.

SUMMER

Baba Ghanoush with Pita Chips

Eggplant is one of the easiest vegetables to grow in the garden. It requires a minimal amount of attention and is a prolific plant. The blossom that becomes the fruit is a striking purple flower that adds a burst of color to the green leaves around it. This classic Mediterranean recipe is great with pita crackers for an hors d'oeuvre or as a sandwich spread for grilled vegetables, chicken, or lamb.

SERVES 4 TO 6

6 pita breads

1^1/$_2$ pounds (about 2 small) globe eggplants

2 cloves garlic, minced

3 tablespoons chopped cilantro

^{1}/$_4$ teaspoon ground cumin

Pinch of cayenne pepper

3 tablespoons extra virgin olive oil

2 teaspoons fresh lemon juice

Kosher salt

Preheat the oven to 350°. Light and heat a charcoal grill to medium-high heat.

Stack the pita breads on top of each other and cut into 6 wedges. Separate each wedge into 2 pieces. Spread the wedges out on a baking sheet and bake for 20 to 30 minutes, until crisp.

Puncture the eggplants in several places with a fork and place on the grill. Cook, uncovered, turning occasionally, for 25 to 30 minutes, until all sides are evenly charred and the eggplants begin to shrivel and collapse. (The eggplants can be baked in a 400° oven for 45 minutes as an alternative method.) Transfer to a cutting board to cool.

Peel the eggplant, coarsely chop the flesh, and transfer to a food processor. Add the garlic, cilantro, cumin, and cayenne and purée. Add the olive oil and lemon juice and pulse to combine. Season to taste with salt. Serve with the pita bread crackers or store, refrigerated, in an airtight container (let sit at room temperature for 1 hour before serving).

Enjoy with Cakebread Cellars Rubaiyat or another slightly chilled, light, flavorful dry red wine or a crisp, fruity rosé.

SUMMER

Marinated Olives

Although Napa Valley is a popular location for olive growing, surprisingly there isn't anyone here curing olives commercially. What makes this even more ironic is that olives of almost any type are a wonderful accompaniment to a glass of wine. This recipe includes two marinades that add extra zing to a bowl of olives. In both recipes, brine-cured olives are used. Before you begin, taste the olives you plan to use. If they taste excessively salty, soak them in warm water for 30 minutes to leach out some of the salt. Once marinated, the olives can be refrigerated in a sealed container for up to one week, making them a handy snack to be enjoyed with a glass of wine before dinner.

SERVES 4 TO 6

NIÇOISE OLIVES WITH ORANGE AND ROSEMARY

$^1/_2$ cup fresh orange juice

2 ($^1/_2$-inch) lengths orange zest

1 clove garlic, smashed

2 cups niçoise olives

1 teaspoon firmly packed whole rosemary leaves

Combine the orange juice, zest, and garlic in a nonreactive saucepan. Bring to a boil over high heat and cook for 5 minutes, until reduced by half. Pour over the olives, add the rosemary, and let sit at room temperature for 1 hour.

PICHOLINE OLIVES WITH HARISSA

$^1/_4$ cup harissa (page 213)

2 cups picholine olives

Prepare the harissa as directed.

Put the olives into a bowl and add the harissa. Toss to coat the olives evenly. Serve cold or at room temperature.

Enjoy with Cakebread Cellars Sauvignon Blanc or a sauvignon blanc that is crisp, dry, and fruity.

Savory Cheese Puffs

Cheese puffs, known as *gougère* in France, are relatively simple to prepare and they can be made in advance and popped in the oven just before guests arrive. They are also very versatile and can be enjoyed with almost any wine. We like them with our Napa Valley Chardonnay, which makes a great aperitif. If you have leftover cheese puffs, serve them instead of bread with dinner.

SERVES 4 TO 6

1 cup water

1/2 cup (1 stick) unsalted butter

1 teaspoon kosher salt

1 cup all-purpose flour

4 large eggs

3/4 cup grated Gruyère

Preheat the oven to 400°. Line a baking sheet with parchment paper.

Bring the water, butter, and salt to a boil in a large, heavy saucepan over medium-high heat. Add the flour all at once and stir until the ingredients form a mass. Continue cooking and stirring for 1 to 2 minutes. Remove from the heat and transfer to the bowl of an electric mixer fitted with a paddle. (This can also be done by hand with a whisk.) Let cool for 2 to 3 minutes. With the mixer running, add the eggs, one at a time, until each is fully incorporated. Add 1/2 cup of the Gruyère and stir just to combine.

Transfer the dough to a pastry bag fitted with a 1/2-inch tip. Pipe golf-ball size mounds 1 inch apart on the prepared baking sheet. Sprinkle with the remaining 1/4 cup Gruyère. Bake for 20 to 25 minutes, until golden brown. Serve warm or at room temperature.

Enjoy with Cakebread Cellars Napa Valley Chardonnay or a chardonnay that has a fresh taste and a silky finish.

FALL

Bruschetta with Wild Mushrooms

Every year at our American Harvest Workshop the visiting chefs fall in love with the selection of mushrooms that Malcolm Clark, Chris Bailey, and Richard Wu, the partners of Gourmet Mushrooms, bring to woo them. Located in the town of Sebastopol, in western Sonoma County, Gourmet Mushrooms cultivates a wide selection of fungi, including shiitake, oyster, and trumpet royale. They also maintain a network of wild mushroom buyers and pickers, allowing them to market an assortment of more exotic types like morels, chanterelles, and hedgehogs. This recipe benefits from a selection of the best mushrooms you can find. If the selection is limited where you live, the dried porcini or even the common button mushrooms will taste wonderful.

SERVES 4 TO 6

$^1/_4$ ounce dried porcini mushrooms

$^1/_2$ cup hot water

6 tablespoons extra virgin olive oil plus additional for brushing

1$^1/_2$ pounds assorted fresh mushrooms (such as oyster, shiitake, cremini), cleaned, stemmed, and thinly sliced

Kosher salt

Freshly ground black pepper

4 cloves garlic

6 ($^1/_2$-inch-thick) slices sweet batard or country-style bread

1 tablespoon chopped flat-leaf parsley, for garnish

Light and heat a charcoal grill to high heat.

Put the porcini in a small bowl and cover with the water. Let sit for 20 minutes. Transfer the porcini to a cutting board and chop into a coarse mixture. Strain the soaking liquid through a fine-mesh sieve and set aside.

Heat a large skillet over high heat. Add the olive oil and fresh mushrooms and cook for 1 to 2 minutes. Add a pinch of salt and pepper and cook for 1 minute. Chop 3 cloves of the garlic and add to the skillet. Add the porcini and cook for 1 to 2 minutes, until the garlic softens. Stir in the reserved liquid from the porcini. Cook for 1 minute, until the liquid is absorbed by the mushrooms.

Grill the bread for 10 to 20 seconds per side, until golden brown. Cut the remaining garlic clove in half and rub the cut side over the bread. Brush the bread with olive oil. Spread equal amounts of the mushrooms over the bread and cut each slice into three pieces. Sprinkle with the parsley and serve.

Enjoy with Cakebread Cellars Napa Valley Chardonnay or a chardonnay with nuances of rich, toasty oak aromas and fresh fruit flavors.

FALL

Roasted Mussels with Bread Crumbs and Garlic

The key to cooking mussels is to buy the freshest available and to serve them the same day. A rule of thumb is to never eat mussels that are already opened before cooking or those that don't open during cooking because they are spoiled and will make you ill. One of the easiest ways to remove the mussel from the shells is to gently scrape it with a teaspoon, being careful not to break the shell, which can be fragile. You can also prepare this dish with clams.

SERVES 4 TO 6

Rock salt

2 pounds (about 18) mussels

1/3 cup dry white wine (such as sauvignon blanc)

1/4 cup extra virgin olive oil

1 clove garlic, minced

1/4 cup dry bread crumbs (page 215)

1 tablespoon minced flat-leaf parsley

Kosher salt

Preheat the oven to 500°.

Fill a large baking sheet with 1/4 inch of rock salt. (The pan should be large enough to hold the mussels in a single layer.) Set aside.

Rinse the mussels and place in a large bowl of cold water. Remove the beard and scrub the shells to remove any sand and barnacles. Discard any mussels that are open. Rinse again.

Pour the wine into a wide skillet with a tight-fitting lid and bring to a boil over high heat. Add the mussels, cover, and cook, shaking the pan every now and then, for 2 to 3 minutes, until the shells open. (If not all of the shells are open, remove those that are and return the unopened mussels to the heat for 1 to 2 minutes. Discard any that remain closed.) Transfer immediately to a wide, shallow dish or separate baking sheet to cool.

Remove the mussels from the shells by gently pulling the meat away from the shells. Separate the shells. Save one half and discard the other. Rinse the saved shells and set aside. Set the mussels in a bowl. (At this point you can put the mussels into a clean container, cover with the juices from the pan, cover with plastic wrap, and refrigerate for up to 1 day.)

Combine the olive oil and garlic in a small saucepan and heat over medium heat for 2 to 3 minutes, until the garlic is soft and the flavors are released without browning. Remove from the heat.

Place the rock salt–filled baking sheet in the oven. Combine the bread crumbs and parsley in a small bowl. Add 1 tablespoon of the oil from the garlic and a pinch of kosher salt. Stir to combine. Set aside.

Spread the shells on a baking sheet and place a mussel in each shell. Sprinkle a small spoonful of the bread crumb mixture over the top of each mussel. Remove the baking sheet of rock salt from the oven and arrange the filled mussel shells over the rock salt. Drizzle with the remaining garlic oil and bake for about 5 minutes, until the bread crumbs begin to turn brown and crisp. Remove from the oven and spoon some of the warm rock salt onto a serving dish. Arrange the mussels on the dish and serve.

Enjoy with Cakebread Cellars Sauvignon Blanc or a crisp, steely white wine with citrus notes.

🦋 FALL

Mushroom Caps Stuffed with Leeks and Fromage Blanc

Cakebread Cellars was once a cow pasture, as was much of Napa Valley. Today the closest dairy farmers are in the southwestern area of Sonoma County. One that we are particularly fond of is Bellwether Farms. Cindy Callahan and her two sons, Liam and Brett, produce outstanding sheep's milk and cow's milk cheeses at Bellwether, including fromage blanc. It is a fresh, tangy cheese, not unlike fresh ricotta. In fact, you can use ricotta as a substitute for fromage blanc in this recipe. Just wrap the ricotta in cheesecloth and hang it over a bowl in the refrigerator overnight to eliminate any excess moisture.

SERVES 4 TO 6

1 large leek, white part only, julienned (2 cups)

2 tablespoons extra virgin olive oil

1/2 teaspoon kosher salt plus additional for seasoning

4 ounces fromage blanc

2 tablespoons finely grated Parmigiano-Reggiano

Freshly ground black pepper

18 large cremini mushrooms, wiped clean and stemmed

White truffle oil (optional)

Preheat the oven to 400°. Brush a baking sheet with olive oil.

Heat the leeks and olive oil in a small sauté pan over medium heat. Add the 1/2 teaspoon salt. Cook, stirring often to prevent browning, for 8 to 10 minutes, until wilted and tender, but not browned. Transfer to a small bowl and let cool.

Add the fromage blanc and Parmigiano to the leeks and stir to mix well. Season with salt and pepper. Scoop up about 1 heaping teaspoon of the mixture and spoon into the bottom of the mushrooms. Set on the prepared baking sheet. Bake in the top third of the oven for 10 to 12 minutes, until the cheese mixture begins to brown and the mushrooms become tender to the bite. Transfer to a serving plate and drizzle with a few drops of truffle oil.

Enjoy with Cakebread Cellars Napa Valley Chardonnay or a chardonnay with great structure and rich fruit flavors.

FALL

Ig's Cheese Crisps

One bite of these crunchy crisps and all other salty snacks will lose their appeal by comparison. You'll never be able to eat just one. The dry jack cheese we use for this recipe is *mezzo secco*, a partially dried cheese from Vella Cheese Company in Sonoma. Ig Vella, the namesake of this recipe, is the son of the company's founder, Tom Vella. Ig's father first began making *mezzo secco* in the 1930s, when he started his company, but production stopped until a few years ago when Ig restored his father's legacy. If you can't find dry jack, Parmigiano-Reggiano can be used. Be careful not to overcook the crisps or they will taste bitter.

SERVES 4 TO 6

1 tablespoon extra virgin olive oil
8 ounces dry jack cheese, grated

Preheat the oven to 375°. Brush a nonstick baking sheet with the olive oil. (After the first batch is baked, the cheese will release its oil, so no need to brush the baking sheet again.)

Place a 3$\frac{1}{2}$-inch pastry ring on the edge of the baking sheet and spread a heaping tablespoon of the cheese in the center of the ring. Repeat until the whole baking sheet is filled. Bake for about 10 minutes, until pale golden. Be careful not to overcook. Remove from the baking sheet with a metal spatula and set on a rolling pin. Gently bend around the rolling pin to create a shape like a potato chip and then gently place on a serving dish. Repeat until all of the cheese is used.

Enjoy with Cakebread Cellars Napa Valley Chardonnay or a chardonnay that is fruit-forward with a long, smooth finish.

WINTER

Dungeness Crab and Watermelon Radish Tostadas with Guacamole

The simplicity of these crab tostadas is their virtue. The crab must be fresh because it takes center stage. Watermelon radishes, a round, green radish between three and four inches in diameter, are some of the last to mature. They are milder tasting than table radishes and have a pretty, pale red center. If you can't find watermelon radishes, you can use a daikon radish, which is about the same size in diameter.

SERVES 4 TO 6

1 watermelon or daikon radish (about 4 ounces or a 2-inch length), peeled

CRAB

$^1/_2$ pound Dungeness crabmeat, picked over for shells and squeezed to remove any excess liquid

2 tablespoons extra virgin olive oil

2 tablespoons fresh lime juice

1 tablespoon coarsely chopped cilantro

1 small serrano chile, finely minced ($^1/_2$ teaspoon)

$^1/_4$ teaspoon finely minced lime zest

GUACAMOLE

1 large ripe avocado, diced

1 tablespoon fresh lime juice

1 small serrano chile, finely minced ($^1/_2$ teaspoon)

Kosher salt

2 romaine lettuce leaves, cut into a fine shred

Cut the radish into paper-thin slices with a mandoline or a sharp knife. Put in an ice water bath until ready to use.

To make the crab mixture: Combine the crabmeat, olive oil, lime juice, cilantro, serrano chile, and lime zest in a small bowl.

To make the guacamole: Put the avocado, lime juice, serrano chile, and a pinch of salt in a small bowl. Mash together with a fork until mixed well, but not too smashed. Arrange the radish slices on a flat surface and place $^1/_2$ teaspoon of the avocado mixture in the center on each. Top with 1 teaspoon of the crab mixture and a little of the romaine.

Enjoy with Cakebread Cellars Sauvignon Blanc or a dry, crisp, and fruity sauvignon blanc.

Bruschetta with Black Mission Figs and Gorgonzola

We are incredibly lucky to have struck up a friendship with the Waltenspiels of Timber Crest Farms many years ago. Located in Healdsburg in Sonoma County, Timber Crest was a pioneer in the organic farm movement and they employ the strictest of growing practices to ensure that all of their fruits and vegetables are grown without chemicals. The Waltenspiels' fruits and vegetables, like the dried figs used in this recipe, are tree ripened and dried naturally. The fig purée can be made in advance and refrigerated for up to one month.

SERVES 4 TO 6

1 1/2 cups dry red wine (such as merlot)

8 ounces dried black mission figs, stemmed and halved

1 bay leaf

1/4 teaspoon anise seed

1/2 loaf country-style bread, cut into 1/2-inch-thick slices

1/2 cup crumbled Gorgonzola

2 tablespoons chopped flat-leaf parsley

Preheat the broiler.

Combine the wine, figs, bay leaf, and anise seed in a small saucepan. Bring to a simmer over medium heat. Cook for 10 minutes, until the figs are rehydrated and soft. Remove from the heat and let cool. Remove the bay leaf, transfer to a food processor, and purée. At this point you can store the mixture in an airtight container, refrigerated, for up to one month.

Put the bread slices on a baking sheet and place under the broiler for 2 minutes per side, until golden brown. Spread a thin layer of the fig purée over the bread slices. Crumble the Gorgonzola and spread equal amounts atop the fig purée on each bruschetta. Place under the broiler for 1 to 2 minutes, until the cheese begins to melt. Cut each slice into 3 pieces on the diagonal, sprinkle with the parsley, and serve.

Enjoy with Cakebread Cellars Merlot or a merlot with fruit-forward aromas and flavors.

WINTER

Soups & Salads

Watercress, Fennel, and Blood Orange Salad

This refreshing salad makes use of blood oranges, which are available at the end of winter and beginning of spring. Blood oranges are a particularly good ingredient in a salad because they are more tangy than sweet, so you can rely on their juices to flavor the salad and add extra zest to the vinaigrette in addition to vinegar.

SERVES 4 TO 6

4 blood oranges

1 tablespoon red wine vinegar

2 shallots, minced

Kosher salt

Freshly ground black pepper

2 fennel bulbs, halved, cored, and cut into thin slices lengthwise

2 bunches watercress

2 heads Belgian endive, chopped

1/2 cup extra virgin olive oil

3 radishes, thinly sliced

Cut the tops and bottoms off the oranges and carefully trim away the rind with a paring knife. Cut into the membrane on both sides of each segment to remove just the segment; do this over a bowl to catch the juices. Set the segments aside and squeeze the membrane to release any remaining juice into the bowl. Set aside.

Pour 2 tablespoons of the orange juice into a small bowl and add the vinegar and shallots. Add a pinch of salt and pepper. Let sit for 20 minutes.

Combine the fennel, watercress, and endive in large bowl. Whisk the olive oil into the orange juice–vinegar mixture in a slow, steady stream. Pour over the greens and toss to coat. Divide among 4 to 6 serving plates and top with the orange segments and radishes.

Enjoy with Cakebread Cellars Sauvignon Blanc or a dry, crisp, light sauvignon blanc.

SPRING

Roasted Beet Salad with Candied Walnuts

Beets are one of the most prolific vegetables in the garden, and since they are one of my favorites, we serve this salad often at the winery. It is crunchy, in large part because of the endive. The Belgian endive we use is from a specialized farmer, Richard Collins, of California Vegetable Specialties, who grows chicory in the California Delta, southeast of Napa. After we met Richard, we asked him to participate in our American Harvest Workshop and every year he arrives with the most beautiful and flavorful heads of endive for the chefs. It's such a versatile vegetable that it has made its way into salads to be eaten fresh, onto the grill for quick cooking, and into roasting pans for braising.

SERVES 4 TO 6

1 cup candied walnuts (page 211)

1^1/$_2$ pounds small assorted beets (such as Chioggia, golden, red)

2 tablespoons sherry vinegar

1 large shallot, minced

Kosher salt

Freshly ground black pepper

2 bunches watercress

2 heads Belgian endive, chopped

1 head frisée, cut into 2-inch lengths

^{1}/$_2$ cup extra virgin olive oil

Prepare the walnuts as directed.

Preheat the oven to 400°.

Wrap the beets in aluminum foil (if using an assortment of beets, wrap separately to prevent the colors from bleeding) and bake for 45 minutes to 1 hour, until tender when pierced with the tip of a knife. Let cool.

While the beets are cooking, make the vinaigrette. Combine the vinegar and shallot in a small bowl. Add a pinch of salt and pepper. Let sit for 20 minutes.

Peel the beets by gently rubbing the skin away with your fingers. Cut each beet into 4 or 6 wedges. Put in a large bowl and add the watercress, endive, and frisée. Whisk the olive oil into the vinegar mixture in a slow, steady stream. Pour over the beets and lettuces and toss to coat evenly. Divide among 4 to 6 chilled serving plates and sprinkle with the nuts.

Enjoy with Cakebread Cellars Sauvignon Blanc or a dry sauvignon blanc that has a good balance of acid and fruit.

SPRING

Piquillo Pepper, Serrano Ham, and Artichoke Salad

The vivid colors of this salad are the results of showcasing a combination of savory Spanish ingredients, including piquillo peppers, which are small red peppers that are roasted, peeled, and preserved in their own juices. The piquillo's flavor varies from mild to subtly spicy. Piquillos can usually be found in gourmet markets that sell imported foods.

SERVES 4 TO 6

$1/2$ cup pine nuts

2 cups water

2 cups dry white wine (such as sauvignon blanc)

2 strips lemon zest

2 cloves garlic, smashed

1 teaspoon kosher salt plus additional for seasoning

1 bay leaf

8 baby artichokes

2 tablespoons sherry vinegar

Freshly ground black pepper

4 ounces loosely packed baby spinach or arugula

1 small head frisée, chopped

5 large piquillo peppers, cut into $1/2$-inch-wide strips lengthwise

3 small spring onions, thinly sliced ($1/4$ cup)

$1/3$ cup extra virgin olive oil

2 ounces thinly sliced Serrano ham, torn into bite-sized pieces

Preheat the oven to 400°.

Spread the pine nuts out on a baking sheet and bake for 5 to 7 minutes, until aromatic and slightly browned.

Combine the water, wine, lemon zest, 1 clove of the garlic, 1 teaspoon salt, and bay leaf in a large saucepan. Cut the stems away from the artichokes. Cut off one-third of the tops, and remove the tough outer leaves to get to the pale yellow-green centers. Add to the saucepan, cover with a small plate to keep submerged, and bring to a boil over high heat. Reduce the heat and cook on a low simmer for 15 minutes, until tender when pierced in the center with a knife. Remove from the heat and let cool in the liquid.

While the artichokes are cooling, combine the vinegar and the remaining clove of garlic in a small bowl. Add a pinch of salt and pepper. Let sit for 20 minutes.

Drain the artichokes and cut into quarters. Put in a large bowl and add the pine nuts, spinach, frisée, peppers, and spring onions. Remove the garlic from the vinegar mixture and discard. Whisk the olive oil into the vinegar mixture in a slow, steady stream. Pour over the salad and toss to coat evenly. Arrange the ham over the salad and serve.

Enjoy with Cakebread Cellars Sauvignon Blanc or a dry sauvignon blanc that expresses hints of citrus in its aromas and flavors.

🌸 SPRING

Winery Events Coordinator George Knopp setting up the dining room in the winery house.

Spring Pea and Lettuce Soup with Ricotta Gnocchi

This is a Napa Valley version of chicken soup with light, delicate gnocchi in place of the proverbial matzo ball. The gnocchi add just the right amount of substance to this otherwise light spring vegetable soup. If you don't have access to fresh peas, frozen are a good substitute.

SERVES 4 TO 6

SOUP

2 tablespoons extra virgin olive oil

2 carrots, peeled and cut into $1/4$-inch dice

1 small leek, white part only, cut into $1/4$-inch dice

1 small yellow onion, cut into $1/4$-inch dice

1 celery stalk, cut into $1/4$-inch dice

2 cloves garlic, minced

6 cups chicken stock (page 212)

1 cup spring peas

2 tablespoons chopped flat-leaf parsley

GNOCCHI

1 cup ricotta

$1/2$ cup freshly grated Parmigiano-Reggiano

1 egg yolk

$1/2$ teaspoon minced lemon zest

$1/4$ cup all-purpose flour (more may be needed, depending on the moisture content of the ricotta)

1 tablespoon chopped flat-leaf parsley

$1/2$ teaspoon kosher salt

1 (4-ounce) head butter lettuce, ribs removed, chopped coarsely

Freshly grated Parmigiano-Reggiano, for garnish

To make the soup: Combine the olive oil, carrots, leek, onion, celery, and garlic in a large saucepan. Cook over medium heat for 5 minutes, until softened. Add the stock, bring to a low boil, and cook for 20 minutes.

To make the gnocchi: Combine the ricotta, Parmigiano, egg yolk, and lemon zest in a bowl. Stir until thoroughly combined. Stir in the flour, parsley, and salt. Mix thoroughly. Take a handful of the mixture and, using the palms of your hands, roll back and forth on a floured surface to form a cylinder slightly smaller than the diameter of a dime. Cut into 1-inch-long pieces. Set on a floured baking sheet. Set aside.

Bring a wide-bottomed pot of salted water to a simmer over medium heat.

Add the peas and parsley to the soup and cook for 5 minutes on medium heat.

When the water comes to a boil, add the gnocchi and cook for about 3 minutes, until the gnocchi rise to the top and become plump. Transfer to the soup with a slotted spoon. Add the lettuce, ladle into bowls, sprinkle with the Parmigiano, and serve.

Enjoy with Cakebread Cellars Napa Valley Chardonnay or Chardonnay Reserve, or a rich, silky chardonnay.

SPRING

Carrot Soup with Garam Masala and Fromage Blanc

Fromage blanc is a fresh cheese that is nearly fat free. It tastes a little like fresh ricotta with the tang of sour cream. In this recipe it's a nice contrast to the creamy carrot soup and the flavors of the garam masala, an Indian spice blend. There are two producers in Northern California that make fromage blanc, Cowgirl Creamery and Bellwether Farms. The cheeses vary slightly in texture and taste as will cheeses from other producers. If these brands aren't available where you live, seek out a local producer for the best product.

SERVES 4 TO 6

2 yellow onions, halved and thinly sliced

1 tart apple (pippin or Granny Smith), peeled, cored, and thinly sliced

2 tablespoons extra virgin olive oil

2 pounds carrots, peeled and thinly sliced

2 teaspoons garam masala or curry powder

6 cups chicken stock (page 212)

2 teaspoons kosher salt plus additional for seasoning

Freshly ground black pepper

$1/2$ cup fromage blanc, at room temperature

1 tablespoon chopped fresh chives, for garnish

Combine the onion, apple, and olive oil in a large saucepan. Heat over high heat and cook for 3 minutes, until softened. Add the carrots and garam masala. Cook for 1 minute. Add the chicken stock and the 2 teaspoons salt. Bring to a boil, reduce the heat to low, and cook uncovered on a low simmer for 20 minutes, or until the carrots are tender.

Transfer to a blender. Put the lid on the blender and remove the vent cover on top. Cover the vent with a towel to release steam. Purée, in batches, until smooth. Return to a saucepan and heat over medium-high heat until warmed through. Season to taste with salt and pepper. Ladle into serving bowls. Add a dollop of fromage blanc and sprinkle with the chives.

Enjoy with Cakebread Cellars Napa Valley Chardonnay or an equally fruit-forward chardonnay.

❧

American Harvest Workshop Recipe

Thomas Moran's Cheese Soufflé with Frisée and Dried Cherries

We welcomed Thomas Moran, the executive chef of Washington, Connecticut's, Mayflower Inn to the 2000 workshop. His fun-with-food philosophy has brought him accolades throughout his cooking career, which he began with a formal education at the Culinary Institute of America and has maintained at some of the country's foremost hotels and resorts. This recipe is an adaptation of the soufflé he served in place of a cheese course at the workshop. He wanted to showcase the many cheese purveyors that he has been introduced to and also use the wonderful nut oils produced by another of the workshop's purveyors, the California Press. This recipe is also a great way to use up the leftover bits of cheese in the refrigerator that might otherwise be overlooked.

SERVES 6

Dry bread crumbs (page 215)

2 tablespoons unsalted butter

3 tablespoons all-purpose flour

$^3/_4$ cup milk

3 egg, separated

$^1/_2$ teaspoon kosher salt plus additional for seasoning

Pinch of nutmeg

$^1/_4$ cup plus 2 tablespoons grated dry jack cheese

$^1/_4$ cup grated Gouda

2 tablespoons fromage blanc

2 tablespoons fresh orange juice

$^1/_2$ cup extra virgin olive oil

Freshly ground black pepper

1 large head frisée, outer leaves discarded

1 cup dried cherries

$^1/_2$ cup pistachios, toasted and coarsely chopped

$^1/_4$ cup pistachio oil (optional)

Preheat the oven to 350°. Butter the sides and bottoms of six 4-ounce ramekins. Coat with bread crumbs. Set aside. Lightly butter a baking sheet and set aside.

Melt the butter over medium heat. Stir in the flour until a smooth paste forms. Add the milk and cook for 3 to 4 minutes, stirring constantly, until thick and smooth. Remove from the heat and stir in the egg yolks, the $^1/_2$ teaspoon salt, and the nutmeg. Transfer to a bowl and place a piece of plastic wrap directly on top of the mixture. Let cool to room temperature.

Add the ¹/₄ cup dry jack, Gouda, and fromage blanc to the milk mixture. Beat the egg whites until stiff peaks form. Fold one-quarter of the egg whites into the cheese mixture to lighten it, then fold the remaining egg whites into that mixture and divide among the prepared ramekins. Place in a large pan and fill halfway up the sides of the ramekins with hot water. Bake for 20 minutes, until firm. Remove the ramekins from the water bath. Let cool for 2 to 3 minutes. Using a kitchen towel to hold the ramekins, gently invert the soufflés into your hand and set top-side up on the prepared baking sheet. Sprinkle with the 2 tablespoons dry jack cheese.

Increase the oven temperature to 450°.

Whisk together the orange juice and olive oil in a small bowl. Add a pinch of salt and pepper and whisk until fully incorporated. Divide the frisée among the serving plates and drizzle with the dressing. Sprinkle with equal amounts of cherries and pistachios. Drizzle the pistachio oil around the plate.

Bake the soufflés for 5 minutes, until slightly browned. Do not bake longer or the soufflés will begin to fall. Arrange a soufflé in the center of each plate and serve immediately.

Enjoy with Cakebread Cellars Benchland Select or an equally complex cabernet sauvignon that is lush and robustly fruity.

SPRING

Niçoise Salad

This salad is named for Nice, the city situated on the French Riviera. *À la niçoise* is a French term used to describe dishes that are cooked in the style of Nice, which include ingredient combinations of tomatoes, anchovies, new potatoes, and basil. Many people associate a niçoise salad with canned tuna, but we think it tastes much better with fresh tuna. The lettuces that we favor are from the Forni-Brown-Welsh gardens in Calistoga.

SERVES 4 TO 6

6 (1-inch-thick) pieces tuna (about 4 ounces each)

1/3 cup plus 2 tablespoons extra virgin olive oil

Kosher salt

Freshly ground black pepper

2 tablespoons red wine vinegar

1 clove garlic, smashed

1 pound green beans or haricot vert, trimmed

1 pound small new potatoes

4 eggs

8 ounces mixed lettuces (such as red oak, mizuna, frisée)

1 fennel bulb, halved, cored, and thinly sliced lengthwise

4 to 6 small ripe tomatoes, cut into wedges

2 radishes, sliced thin

1/2 cup niçoise olives

2 tablespoons torn basil leaves

Heat a nonstick skillet over high heat. Rub the tuna with the 2 tablespoons olive oil. Sprinkle with salt and pepper. Add to the skillet and cook for 2 to 3 minutes per side, until seared on the outside but still slightly pink in the center. Transfer to a plate and refrigerate until ready to use.

Combine the vinegar, garlic, and a pinch of salt and pepper in a small bowl. Let sit for 20 minutes.

Bring a large saucepan of salted water to a boil over high heat. Add the green beans and cook for 2 to 3 minutes, until al dente. Transfer to an ice water bath with tongs or a slotted spoon. Drain the green beans and set aside.

Put the potatoes in a saucepan and cover with cold water. Add a pinch of salt and bring to a boil over high heat. Decrease the heat and cook on a simmer for 12 minutes, until tender when pierced with a fork. Drain. Cut into quarters and put in a small bowl.

While the potatoes are cooking, put the eggs in a small saucepan and cover with cold water. Add a generous pinch of salt and bring to a boil over medium-high heat. Cook for 12 minutes. Run under cold water until cool. Peel and cut the eggs into quarters lengthwise. Set aside.

Whisk the 1/3 cup olive oil into the vinegar mixture in a slow, steady stream.

Put the lettuces in a large, shallow, decorative serving bowl. Add the fennel and toss to combine. Break the tuna into large flakes and arrange over the greens. Arrange the potatoes, eggs, tomatoes, green beans, and radishes over the top of the tuna. Sprinkle the olives around the sides of the bowl. Drizzle the vinaigrette over the salad mixture and top with the basil. Divide among serving plates.

Enjoy with Cakebread Cellars Sauvignon Blanc or a dry, crisp, fruity sauvignon blanc.

SUMMER

Watermelon and Pickled Red Onion Salad with Mint and Feta

Visitors are always surprised to find watermelon in the garden. During the summer when melons are at the peak of their season, we grow several types, including a yellow watermelon that is very pretty inside and an heirloom called Moon and Stars, which got its name from the markings on the outside of the rind. This salad is made with red watermelon, which adds a crunchy texture and a sweet foil to the bite of red onion and the tangy feta cheese.

SERVES 4 TO 6

2 small red onions, cut into $1/4$-inch-thick slices

$1/2$ cup water

$1/2$ cup red wine vinegar

$1/4$ cup sugar

4 pounds seedless watermelon

4 ounces baby arugula

1 small head radicchio, chopped

$1/4$ cup extra virgin olive oil

4 ounces feta, crumbled

2 teaspoons chopped fresh mint

Separate the rings of the onion and put in a stainless steel or glass bowl. Bring the water, vinegar, and sugar to a boil in a small saucepan over high heat. Pour over the onion rings and let steep for 30 minutes in the refrigerator, stirring occasionally.

Cut the watermelon in half lengthwise. Set on a cutting surface and cut the rind away, starting with a thin slice across the top with a sharp knife, creating a flat surface. Cut the rind away in strips starting at the edge of the top and slicing down toward the cutting board. Discard the rind. Cut the watermelon into 1-inch chunks. Set aside.

Combine the arugula and radicchio in a bowl. Drain the onions, reserving the liquid, and add the onions and watermelon to the arugula and radicchio. Combine 2 tablespoons of the reserved liquid with the olive oil and drizzle over the salad. Toss gently with your hands. Sprinkle with the feta and mint. Divide the salad among 4 to 6 chilled plates. Serve immediately.

Enjoy with Cakebread Cellars Sauvignon Blanc or a dry, crisp sauvignon blanc.

SUMMER

Cakebread's Garden Tomato and Bread Salad

When I first began my garden there was a limited selection of tomato seeds and plants available. In the ensuing thirty years there has been a staggering growth in the availability of heirloom fruits and vegetables. We grow as many as seventeen types of tomatoes in the garden, many of which are prized heirlooms. A variety of heirloom tomatoes in this salad adds a brilliant color palette as well as a mixture of flavors and texture. Use as many different types as you can for the best taste.

SERVES 4 TO 6

$1/2$ loaf (about $1/2$ pound) stale country-style bread, cut into 1-inch-thick slices

1 large clove garlic, peeled and halved

2 pounds assorted ripe heirloom tomatoes (such as Cherokee Purple, Green Zebra, Brandywine, Marvel Striped, Black Prince), cut into 1-inch chunks

$1/2$ cup extra virgin olive oil

$1/4$ cup balsamic vinegar

1 tablespoon torn fresh basil leaves plus additional sprigs for garnish

Kosher salt

Freshly ground black pepper

1 head radicchio, leaves separated

Preheat the broiler.

Set the bread on a baking sheet and place under the broiler. Cook for 1 to 2 minutes per side, until golden brown. Turn off the oven and remove the baking sheet. Rub both sides of the bread slices lightly with the cut side of the garlic clove. Cut the bread into generous 1-inch cubes, spread out on a baking sheet, and return to the oven. Let sit with the oven off and the oven door closed for 20 to 30 minutes, until the croutons are slightly dried.

Combine the tomatoes, olive oil, and vinegar in a large bowl. (At this point, you can let the tomatoes sit at room temperature for up to 2 hours before serving.) Add the torn basil and stir to mix. Add the bread and toss to coat. Season to taste with salt and pepper. Let sit for 10 minutes so that the bread absorbs the juices from the tomatoes.

Arrange the large radicchio leaves on 4 to 6 serving plates and top each with equal amounts of the bread salad. Garnish with a sprig of the basil.

Enjoy with Cakebread Cellars Sauvignon Blanc or a dry sauvignon blanc that has a nice balance of acid and fruit.

SUMMER

Spanish-Inspired Salad of Roasted Peppers and Charred Eggplant

In late summer, when the garden and markets are bursting with peppers and eggplants, this dish puts them to great use. The peppers and eggplants are roasted over a charcoal grill, which imparts a deep, smoky taste. This salad is served at the winery as a side dish with beef or lamb and as a first course.

SERVES 4 TO 6

2 large eggplants (about 1^1/$_2$ pounds each)

4 sweet red peppers (such as bell peppers or pimientos)

^{1}/$_2$ cup extra virgin olive oil

2 teaspoons sherry vinegar

1 clove garlic, mashed to a paste

Kosher salt

Freshly ground black pepper

1 tablespoon chopped fresh basil

Arrange coals on one side of a charcoal grill and light. Heat to high heat.

Put the eggplants and peppers on the grill over indirect heat. Cook, uncovered, for 20 to 25 minutes, until charred on all sides and the eggplants begin to collapse. Turn frequently for even cooking. Transfer to a bowl to cool.

Peel and seed the peppers and cut into ^{1}/$_2$-inch-wide strips. Peel the eggplant and cut into ^{1}/$_2$-inch slices lengthwise. Cut each slice into ^{1}/$_2$-inch-wide strips and arrange on a platter in an alternating pattern with the peppers. Whisk together the olive oil, vinegar, and garlic. Season to taste with salt and pepper. Drizzle over the top of the eggplant and peppers. Sprinkle with the basil and let sit for at least 1 hour at room temperature before serving.

Enjoy with Cakebread Cellars Pinot Noir or Rubaiyat, or any light-bodied, fruity red wine.

❧ SUMMER

Warm Salad of Sea Scallops, Fingerling Potatoes, and Cherry Tomatoes

Jack loves scallops and would eat them every day if he could. Although he's not much of a salad eater, he says this is great for a Saturday afternoon in front of a game because it is so rich and filling. Using a variety of cherry tomatoes makes a very important difference in the flavor and presentation, as does cooking the potatoes until they are very crisp—the crunchy exterior gives the salad its backbone.

SERVES 4 TO 6

$1/2$ pound fingerling or small Yukon gold potatoes

Kosher salt

5 tablespoons extra virgin olive oil

Freshly ground black pepper

2 cups mixed cherry tomatoes, halved

6 ounces mixed lettuces

$1^1/2$ pounds sea scallops, cut into 2-inch pieces

1 tablespoon gremolata (page 212)

2 teaspoons fresh lemon juice

Preheat the oven to 450°.

Put the potatoes in a small saucepan. Cover with cold water and add a pinch of salt. Bring to a boil over high heat. Cook for 12 to 14 minutes, until tender when pierced with a knife. Transfer to a colander to drain. Let cool.

Peel the potatoes and cut in half. Put on a baking sheet and pour 3 tablespoons of the olive oil over the potatoes. Toss to coat evenly. Bake for 20 to 25 minutes, until browned and crispy, stirring occasionally to brown evenly. Season to taste with salt and pepper.

Combine the tomatoes and lettuces in a large serving bowl.

Heat the remaining 2 tablespoons olive oil in a large sauté pan over high heat. Add the scallops and cook for 2 minutes, until evenly browned. Turn and cook the other side for 1 minute. Add the gremolata and gently shake the pan to combine with the scallops. Add to the bowl with the lettuces. Add the potatoes and lemon juice and toss to combine. Divide among 4 to 6 plates and serve.

Enjoy with Cakebread Cellars Napa Valley Chardonnay or an equally rich chardonnay.

SUMMER

Tuscan Tomato and Bread Soup
with Fresh Basil

Tuscany-inspired, this rustic soup relies on the taste of the tomatoes, so they must be very ripe and flavorful. Also, the finishing touch is a splash of olive oil, and the better the olive oil, the better the bowl of soup. We always use our estate extra virgin olive oil, which hints at green grass and has notes of almonds and pepper.

SERVES 4 TO 6

$^1/_4$ cup extra virgin olive oil plus additional
    for drizzling

3 cloves garlic

3 pounds vine-ripened tomatoes, peeled, seeded,
    and diced

3 sprigs basil, leaves and stems separated

1 teaspoon kosher salt

2 cups chicken stock (page 212)

3 ounces stale country-style bread, torn into
    bite-sized pieces

Pinch of sugar (optional)

Heat the $^1/_4$ cup olive oil in a wide-bottom nonreactive pan over medium heat. Add the garlic cloves and cook for 2 minutes, until the oil is infused with flavor. Remove and discard the garlic and add the tomatoes, basil stems, and salt. Cook for 5 minutes, until the tomatoes become soft. Add the stock and bring to a low boil. Add the bread and cook for 20 to 25 minutes, until the bread begins to break apart and the soup begins to thicken. Remove from the heat and let cool to room temperature. Remove and discard the basil stems. If the soup tastes slightly tart add the sugar to bring out the natural sweetness of the tomatoes. Divide the soup among 4 to 6 serving bowls. Tear the basil leaves into small pieces and sprinkle over the top. Drizzle with olive oil.

Enjoy with Cakebread Cellars Sauvignon Blanc or a dry, fruity, crisp sauvignon blanc.

Spanish Red Gazpacho

On a hot summer day, this red gazpacho, served in a very traditional way with chopped Serrano ham and egg white, is a refreshing choice for lunch or a light dinner. It can be prepared ahead of time, which makes it great for summertime entertaining. Serrano ham, a dry-cured ham, can usually be found at gourmet delis. Prosciutto makes a fine substitute.

SERVES 4 TO 6

2 (1-inch-thick) slices stale sweet French bread, crusts removed and cut into cubes

1 large red tomato, peeled, seeded, and chopped ($3/4$ cup)

1 large cucumber, peeled, seeded, and diced (2 cups)

$1/2$ fennel bulb, cored and sliced

1 small red bell pepper, seeded, deveined, and chopped

2 tablespoons sherry vinegar

1 clove garlic, chopped

1 teaspoon kosher salt

$1^1/4$ cups ice water

$1/4$ cup extra virgin olive oil plus additional for garnish

1 hard-boiled egg white, finely diced

1 ounce Serrano ham, finely minced

Put the bread in small bowl and cover with cold water. Let sit for 10 minutes, until softened.

Gently squeeze the bread in your hands to eliminate any excess water and put the bread in a blender. Add the tomato, cucumber, fennel, bell pepper, vinegar, garlic, and salt. Start blending on high and, with the motor running, add the ice water and the $1/4$ cup olive oil. Blend until smooth. Refrigerate for 2 hours, until thoroughly chilled.

Pour into serving bowls and top each with a spoonful of the egg white and ham. Drizzle with a thin stream of olive oil in a decorative pattern.

Enjoy with Cakebread Cellars Sauvignon Blanc or a dry, crisp sauvignon blanc with citrus fruit characteristics.

SUMMER

Chicken Soup with Ancho Chiles, Avocado, and Lime

The saturated colors and abundance of gorgeous ingredients in this soup belie its ethereally light taste. Cooking the chicken first accomplishes two things. One, the cooking time of the chicken is controlled so that it doesn't become overcooked; and two, the liquid it is cooked in then becomes the broth that adds flavor to the soup.

SERVES 4 TO 6

2 chicken breasts

6 cups cold water

$^1/_2$ white onion, cut into wedges

1 teaspoon kosher salt plus additional for seasoning

1 bay leaf

1 whole clove

1 dried ancho chile, stemmed and seeded

8 ripe plum tomatoes

2 cloves garlic, unpeeled

$^1/_2$ teaspoon Mexican oregano

$^1/_4$ teaspoon ground cumin

Freshly ground black pepper

1 avocado, cut into $^1/_2$-inch dice

1 cup finely shredded cabbage

2 radishes, thinly sliced

1 lime, cut into wedges

Put the chicken in a large saucepan. Add the water, onion, salt, bay leaf, and clove and bring to a boil over high heat. Decrease the heat to medium-low and cook on a simmer for 12 minutes. Remove from the heat and let the chicken cool in the liquid. When cool enough to handle, remove the chicken from the broth. Remove and discard the bones and skin. Cut the meat into a $^1/_2$-inch dice and set aside. Strain the broth through a fine-mesh sieve and set aside.

While the chicken is cooking, heat a nonstick skillet over medium heat. Add the chile and cook for about 5 seconds, holding it flat against the pan with a metal spatula. Transfer to a bowl and cover with warm water. Let sit for 15 minutes, until soft.

Add the tomatoes and garlic to the skillet and cook for 5 to 10 minutes, until they begin to blister and blacken. Remove from the heat.

Drain the chile and put in a blender. Peel the garlic and add the garlic to the blender. Add the cooked tomatoes, the oregano, and the cumin. Purée until smooth. Add 2 cups of the reserved liquid from the chicken and continue to purée until incorporated. Transfer to a large saucepan. Add the chicken and cook over medium-high heat until heated through. Season to taste with salt and pepper.

Ladle into warm bowls and top each with a spoonful of avocado, cabbage, and radish. Serve with lime wedges on the side.

Enjoy with Cakebread Cellars Napa Valley Chardonnay or a chardonnay with green apple and pear notes in the aromas and flavors.

SUMMER

Wild Mushrooms, Butternut Squash, and Baby Spinach Salad

In autumn, when the days become shorter and the weather cools down, the garden crops change dramatically and, as a result, so do our menus. When Brian begins to serve this salad, we know that autumn has officially arrived. Farmers' markets are often the best resource for buying a selection of mushrooms. Fresh mushrooms should feel heavy, plump, and supple, and should not be wrinkled or frayed on the edges.

SERVES 4 TO 6

1^1/$_2$ pounds assorted wild mushrooms
    (such as chanterelle, shiitake, or oyster)

2 cups water

2 tablespoons soy sauce

3 cloves garlic

1 sprig thyme

2 pounds butternut squash, peeled and cut into
    ^{1}/$_2$-inch cubes

^{1}/$_3$ cup plus ^{1}/$_4$ cup extra virgin olive oil

Kosher salt

Freshly ground black pepper

1 tablespoon fresh thyme

1 tablespoon fresh lemon juice

^{1}/$_2$ cup walnut oil

5 ounces baby spinach leaves

^{1}/$_2$ head radicchio, torn into bite-sized pieces

1 head Belgian endive, cut into bite-sized pieces

1 ounce dry jack cheese

Preheat the oven to 400°.

Wipe clean and stem the mushrooms, reserving the stems. Cut the caps into 1-inch pieces.

Combine the water, mushroom stems, 1 tablespoon of the soy sauce, 1 of the garlic cloves, and the sprig of thyme in a small saucepan. Bring to a boil over medium heat. Reduce the heat to low and simmer for 30 minutes. Strain the mushroom broth into a clean saucepan.

Spread the squash on a baking dish. Pour the ^{1}/$_4$ cup olive oil over the squash and toss to coat evenly. Sprinkle with salt and pepper. Bake for about 20 minutes, until the center is tender and the outside is browned.

Spread the mushrooms out in a baking dish and drizzle with the ^{1}/$_3$ cup olive oil and the remaining 1 tablespoon soy sauce. Add the thyme leaves. Chop the remaining 2 garlic cloves and add to the mushrooms. Sprinkle with salt and pepper and cover with aluminum foil. Bake for 20 minutes, until the mushrooms are soft. Remove from the oven and remove the foil. If there are any juices in the bottom of the dish, strain them into the mushroom broth.

Increase the oven temperature to 500°. Return the mushrooms to the oven, uncovered, and cook for 10 to 15 minutes, until browned and crisp.

Bring the mushroom broth to a boil over high heat and cook for 10 to 15 minutes, until reduced to one-quarter of the amount. Add the lemon juice. Whisk in the walnut oil.

Combine the spinach, radicchio, and endive in a large bowl. Add the squash, mushrooms, and vinaigrette. Toss to coat. Divide among serving plates and shave the dry jack cheese over the top.

Enjoy with Cakebread Cellars Napa Valley Chardonnay or Rubaiyat as a nice complement to the rich, earthy flavors of the salad. Or select a chardonnay with concentrated fruit flavors or a light-bodied red wine that can be served slightly chilled.

🌸 FALL

Warm Goat Cheese Salad with Pancetta, Shaved Fennel, and Sliced Pears

One of the first purveyors we invited to participate in our American Harvest Workshop was Laura Chenel. Visiting her when she was still making cheese in her garage was one of the most memorable field trips for our visiting chefs. Often credited as the mother of American goat cheese, Laura has been raising goats in Sonoma County since 1979, first in Sebastopol and now on the border of Napa County, in the Carneros district. After an apprenticeship in France where she learned to perfect farmstead cheeses, she returned to Sonoma County and has been making a fine selection of goat cheeses ever since. In this salad we use her fresh goat cheese, which is creamy and soft and melts when the warm dressing is added. This salad wilts quickly, so it should be served immediately.

SERVES 4 TO 6

10 ounces mixed lettuces

1 fennel bulb, cored and thinly sliced lengthwise

1 ripe pear, peeled, cored, halved, and thinly sliced lengthwise

3 ounces fresh goat cheese, crumbled

$1/3$ cup plus 1 tablespoon extra virgin olive oil

4 ounces pancetta, cut into $1/4$-inch dice

2 cloves garlic, minced

4 small tomatoes, peeled, seeded, and diced (1 cup)

$1/4$ cup sherry vinegar

In a large serving bowl, combine the lettuces, fennel, pear, and goat cheese.

Heat a sauté pan over medium heat. Add the 1 tablespoon olive oil and the pancetta and cook for 3 to 5 minutes, until crispy, stirring occasionally. Pour out any excess oil and add the $1/3$ cup olive oil. Add the garlic and cook for 1 minute, until soft. Increase the heat to high. Add the tomatoes and cook for 1 minute. Add the vinegar and bring to a boil. Pour over the greens and quickly toss to coat evenly. Serve family style.

Enjoy with Cakebread Cellars Rubaiyat or a light-bodied wine that offers fresh fruit flavors.

FALL

Sweet Corn, Chanterelle, and Wild Rice Soup with Garlic Croutons

The funny thing about wild rice is that it isn't really rice. It's a native grass that grows in the same wet conditions as rice and has the same grain-like appearance. Its nutty, rustic taste is a great complement to sweet corn and to the woodsy taste of the mushrooms in this soup. The wild rice that we like best is grown by the Lundberg family in Richvale, east of Napa in Yolo County. Lundberg Family Farms has been growing a unique selection of rice for several decades and was one of the first participants in our American Harvest Workshop.

SERVES 4 TO 6

RICE

1/2 yellow onion, minced

2 tablespoons extra virgin olive oil

1/2 cup wild rice

1 cup chicken stock (page 212)

1/2 teaspoon kosher salt

SOUP

2 tablespoons extra virgin olive oil

1 yellow onion, finely diced

2 carrots, peeled and finely diced

2 stalks celery, finely diced

2 ounces prosciutto, finely diced

3 cloves garlic, minced

3 fresh sage leaves

2 cups fresh corn kernels (about 2 ears)

1/2 pound chanterelle mushrooms, cleaned and sliced

5 cups chicken stock (page 212)

Kosher salt

Freshly ground black pepper

CROUTONS

2 cups 1/2-inch crustless bread cubes

2 tablespoons chopped flat-leaf parsley

3 cloves garlic, finely minced

1/4 cup extra virgin olive oil

1/4 teaspoon kosher salt

2 tablespoons chopped flat-leaf parsley

Preheat the oven to 350°.

To make the rice: Combine the onion and olive oil in a small skillet over medium heat. Cook for 2 to 3 minutes, until the onion is soft. Add the wild rice. Stir to coat with the oil. Add the stock and salt. Bring to a boil, cover, decrease the heat to low, and cook on a low simmer for about 1 hour, or until about half of the rice kernels burst.

To prepare the soup: While the rice is cooking, heat a large, wide saucepan over high heat. Add the olive oil, onion, carrots, celery, and prosciutto. Cook for 2 to 3 minutes, until the vegetables begin to soften. Add the garlic and sage. Cook for 1 to 2 minutes to soften the garlic. Add the corn and mushrooms and cook for 1 to 2 minutes, until the mushrooms begin to soften. Add the stock and a pinch of salt and pepper. Bring to a boil, reduce the heat to low, and cook, uncovered, on a low simmer for 20 to 25 minutes, until the vegetables are tender.

To make the croutons: Mix together the bread cubes, parsley, and garlic in a small bowl. Add the olive oil and salt and stir to coat the bread evenly. Spread out into a single layer on a baking sheet and bake for 20 minutes, or until crisp and golden brown, stirring occasionally to brown evenly. Set aside.

Add the rice to the soup and stir to mix well. Add the parsley and ladle into warm bowls. Top with a handful of the croutons and serve.

Enjoy with Cakebread Cellars Napa Valley Chardonnay or a silky, complex chardonnay.

FALL

Butternut Squash Soup with Sherry and Almonds

Butternut squash becomes almost sweet when it reaches maturity. Roasting it concentrates the flavors, which adds to the intensity of this soup's taste. Sherry, a fortified wine that is made in southern Spain, is used to add complexity because it has less acid and more sweetness, but still acts like a bridge between the finished soup and the wine it is served with. A good sherry should be used. Never cook with sherry that you wouldn't drink.

SERVES 4 TO 6

1 large (3^1/2- to 4-pound) butternut squash, halved and seeded

2 cups water

1 large leek, white part only, halved and sliced crosswise

1 large yellow onion, halved and thinly sliced crosswise

2 tablespoons extra virgin olive oil

^{1}/2 cup plus 1 tablespoon medium-dry sherry

2 tablespoons honey

4 cups chicken stock (page 212)

^{1}/2 teaspoon kosher salt

^{1}/4 cup sliced almonds

^{1}/2 cup heavy whipping cream

Pinch of freshly grated nutmeg

1 tablespoon chopped fresh chives

Preheat the oven to 400°.

Arrange the squash, cut side down, on a baking sheet. Add the water and bake, uncovered, for 1 hour, or until the squash is tender when pierced with a knife.

While the squash is cooking, put the leeks in a large bowl and cover with water. Let sit for 5 minutes to let any sand and dirt settle to the bottom. Scoop the leeks out of the bowl and drain. Combine with the onion and olive oil in a small stockpot and heat over medium heat. Cook for about 10 minutes, until tender. Add the ^{1}/2 cup sherry and the honey. Cook for 1 minute. Add the stock and salt. Scoop the squash away from the skin and add to the stockpot. Cook on a simmer for 20 to 30 minutes, until the vegetables are completely soft.

While the soup is cooking, spread the almonds out on a baking sheet and bake for 10 minutes, until slightly browned.

Transfer the vegetables in the soup and all but 1 cup of the broth into a blender. Put the lid on the blender and remove the vent cover on the top. Cover the vent with a towel to release steam. Purée the vegetables, in batches, until smooth, adding the reserved broth as needed. Return to a saucepan to heat over low heat, and stir in ^{1}/4 cup of the cream and the nutmeg.

Whisk together the remaining ^{1}/4 cup cream with the 1 tablespoon sherry in a bowl until soft peaks form.

Divide the soup into soup bowls. Spoon a small amount of the whipped cream into the center, sprinkle with a few almonds, and top with the chives.

Enjoy with Cakebread Cellars Chardonnay Reserve or a rich, complex chardonnay with a creamy, full body.

FALL

Smoked Trout, Escarole, and Celery Root Salad with Poppyseed Dressing

One of the advantages of living in the Napa Valley is that we are surrounded by extremely talented food artisans, including the Cowgirl Creamery cheese makers in Point Reyes, near the Sonoma County coast. Sue Conley and Peggy Smith, owners of Cowgirl Creamery, were devoted to promoting small dairies when they began to make several of their own cheeses. Their crème fraîche is the ingredient that gives this recipe's vinaigrette the richness that is a nice contrast to the smoked trout and escarole. At the peak of its season, escarole has pale yellow-green leaves and a mild taste. If there are any dark leaves, which can be bitter, discard them before chopping the heads.

SERVES 4 TO 6

1/4 cup apple cider vinegar

2 tablespoons crème fraîche

1 shallot, minced

1 scant teaspoon cream-style horseradish

1/4 cup extra virgin olive oil

1 tablespoon poppyseeds

6 cups chopped escarole, pale yellow-green leaves only

2 cups torn radicchio

1 small celery root, peeled

1 tablespoon loosely packed chopped fresh dill

2 (1/4-pound) smoked trout fillets, broken into bite-sized pieces

Whisk together the vinegar, crème fraîche, shallot, and horseradish in a small bowl. While whisking continuously, add the olive oil in a slow, steady stream. Add the poppyseeds.

Combine the escarole and radicchio in a large serving bowl. Shave the celery root with a vegetable peeler into the greens. Add the vinaigrette and dill and toss to mix well. Arrange the trout over the top and serve.

Enjoy with Cakebread Cellars Chardonnay Reserve or an older chardonnay.

WINTER

Curly Endive, Fig, and Blue Cheese Salad with Toasted Walnuts

The pale yellow-green and white curled leaves of curly endive make it easy to identify and are similar to its relatives, frisée and escarole. Curly endive grows year-round, but its peak is in the fall, when it benefits from the colder weather. Its mild taste is the perfect background for the rich figs, blue cheese, and toasted walnuts. Grappa, an alcoholic beverage made from grape pomace, can usually be found at wine shops and liquor stores.

SERVES 4 TO 6

1 cup grappa

8 dried figs, stemmed and cut into $1/4$-inch-thick slices

2 tablespoons apple cider vinegar

1 teaspoon Dijon mustard

1 shallot, minced

Kosher salt

Freshly ground black pepper

6 cups chopped curly endive, tender, pale yellow-green parts only

3 small stalks celery, thinly sliced (1 cup)

1 cup walnuts, toasted

$1/2$ cup (about 3 ounces) crumbled blue cheese

$1/3$ cup walnut oil

Combine the grappa and figs in a small saucepan and bring to a boil over high heat. Cook for 5 minutes, or until the liquid is reduced by half. Let sit for 20 minutes so that the figs absorb the liquid and become soft.

Whisk together the vinegar, mustard, and shallot in a small bowl. Add a pinch of salt and pepper. Let sit for at least 20 minutes.

Combine the endive, celery, walnuts, and blue cheese in a large serving bowl. Drain the figs and add to the bowl. Whisk the walnut oil into the vinegar mixture in a slow, steady stream, until fully incorporated. Pour over the salad mixture, toss to coat evenly, and serve.

Enjoy with Cakebread Cellars Chardonnay Reserve or an older chardonnay with a full body, complex structure, and rich fruit flavors.

WINTER

American Harvest Workshop Recipe

Jan Birnbaum's Spicy Seafood Stew

In 1995 we welcomed Napa Valley's own Jan Birnbaum as a participating chef at our workshop. Jan, a Louisiana native, learned to cook in the company of his mother and aunts as a child and as an adult in the kitchen of Paul Prudhomme. From New Orleans, Jan went to New York and San Francisco, cooking up a storm of rave reviews for his ability to create elegant haute cuisine. In 1994 he returned to his roots when he opened Catahoula, a Louisiana-style restaurant and saloon in Calistoga. This southern-style stew elevates everyday ingredients into a masterpiece of flavor. The night he prepared it he used local clams from Hog Island and tasso—cured, seasoned, smoked pork—from Bruce Aidells of Aidells's Sausage Company. Bruce has been a valued purveyor at many of our workshops.

SERVES 4 TO 6

2 tablespoons extra virgin olive oil

4 ounces tasso or andouille, thinly sliced

1/2 fennel bulb, halved, cored, and thinly sliced

4 shallots, thinly sliced

2 cloves garlic, sliced

1/2 jalapeño, minced

4 ripe tomatoes, peeled, seeded, and diced

1/2 cup dry white wine

2 cups fish stock or water

1 1/2 pounds mussels, debearded, scrubbed, and rinsed

1 pound Manila clams, rinsed

1 1/2 pounds firm-fleshed fish (such as sea bass or Hawaiian snapper), cut into 1-inch pieces

1/2 pound jumbo prawns, peeled and deveined, with tails on

Chopped flat-leaf parsley, for garnish

Heat a large, wide stockpot or large Dutch oven over high heat. Add the olive oil and heat. Add the tasso and cook for 2 to 3 minutes, until browned. Transfer the sausage with a slotted spoon to a small plate. Add the fennel, shallots, garlic, and jalapeño to the pan. Decrease the heat to medium and cook for 5 minutes, until the vegetables soften. Add the tomatoes and wine and cook for about 5 minutes, until the wine is reduced by half. Add the stock, mussels, and clams, cover, and cook for about 5 minutes, until the shells open. Discard any shells that have not opened. Decrease the heat to medium. Add the fish and prawns. Cover and cook for about 10 minutes, until the fish is firm and the prawns are pink. Spoon into bowls. Add a few slices of sausage, sprinkle with the parsley, and serve.

Enjoy with Cakebread Cellars Sauvignon Blanc or a dry, fruity sauvignon blanc.

WINTER

Sandwiches, Pizzas, & Bread

Moroccan Lamb Sandwich
with Yogurt-Mint Sauce

Sandwiches have a long history at Cakebread Cellars. In the early days, I'd make them by the dozens to feed our crew during harvest. Today we don't serve sandwiches for many occasions, but when we do they are always eaten with gusto. This sandwich is in a pita bread pocket, so it is critical that the lamb patties aren't too thick or the whole sandwich can get too big to take a bite. The patties should be small enough that two can fit into each pita pocket and shouldn't be any thicker than half an inch.

SERVES 6

1 cup plain yogurt

2 tablespoons chopped fresh cilantro

1 teaspoon chopped fresh mint

1 clove garlic, mashed into a paste

1 1/2 pounds ground lamb

1 small white onion, grated (1/2 cup)

1 tablespoon minced fresh parsley

2 teaspoons sweet paprika

1 teaspoon kosher salt

1 teaspoon ground cumin

1/4 teaspoon cayenne pepper

3 whole pita breads

6 leaves red or green leaf lettuce

12 thin slices ripe tomato

6 paper-thin slices red onion

1 avocado, diced

Light and heat a charcoal grill to high heat.

Combine the yogurt, 1 tablespoon of the cilantro, the mint, and garlic in a small bowl. Set aside.

Put the lamb, onion, the remaining 1 tablespoon cilantro, the parsley, paprika, salt, cumin, and cayenne in a large bowl. Coat your hands with olive oil and mix the ingredients with your hands until thoroughly incorporated. Shape the mixture into 12 oval patties, 3 inches long and 1/2 inch thick.

Place the patties on the grill and cook for 3 to 4 minutes per side, until browned on the exterior and medium-rare in the center. Transfer to a plate.

Cut the pitas in half and loosen the center to create a pocket. Place a piece of lettuce into each pita, add 2 tomato slices, 1 onion slice, and a spoonful of avocado. Arrange 2 lamb patties inside each pita and top with a spoonful of the yogurt sauce. Serve immediately.

Enjoy with Cakebread Cellars Cabernet Sauvignon or a classic, fruity, spicy cabernet sauvignon or a zinfandel with black pepper on the nose.

SPRING

Chicken Sandwich with Asparagus, Prosciutto, and Mozzarella

Roasting is one of the easiest and best ways to cook asparagus. The spears cook quickly, the flavors intensify, and the texture remains slightly crunchy. Peeling away the bottom of the stalks reveals the tender inside, makes for a better presentation, and ultimately provides a higher yield because less of the tough end of the stalk is discarded.

SERVES 4

16 asparagus stalks, tough end discarded, stalks peeled

4 tablespoons extra virgin olive oil

Kosher salt

Freshly ground black pepper

4 large chicken breasts

4 high-quality bread rolls, split lengthwise

8 paper-thin slices prosciutto

8 ounces fresh mozzarella, thinly sliced

Preheat the oven to 400°.

Arrange the asparagus in a shallow baking dish or ovenproof skillet and add 2 tablespoons of the olive oil. Toss to coat evenly. Sprinkle with salt and pepper and bake for 15 minutes, until tender.

Lay the chicken breasts over a piece of plastic wrap set on a flat surface. Cover with another sheet of plastic wrap and pound out to $1/2$ inch thick with a mallet. Season with salt and pepper. Heat the remaining 2 tablespoons olive oil in a large skillet over medium-high heat. Add the chicken and cook for 2 to 3 minutes per side, until evenly browned. Place a piece of chicken on the bottom half of each roll. Top each with 2 prosciutto slices, 4 asparagus spears, and 1 to 2 mozzarella slices. Place on a baking sheet. Set the top of the bread cut side up on the baking sheet. Place under the broiler for 2 to 3 minutes, until the cheese melts and the tops of the bread are toasted. Place the top half of the bread over the cheese, cut in half, and serve.

Enjoy with Cakebread Cellars Napa Valley Chardonnay or a chardonnay with crisp apple and pear flavors and hints of toasty oak.

SPRING

Pan Bagna

A classic French sandwich, Pan Bagna gets its robust taste from compressing it until the flavors of the ingredients blend into each other. The object set on top of the sandwiches needs to be heavy enough to flatten the sandwiches, and should be carefully arranged so that it doesn't topple off and break anything. The most flavorful canned tuna is imported Italian tuna packed in olive oil. If you don't like anchovies, you can leave them off, but they do add a great salty essence to the sandwich that is balanced by the hard-boiled eggs.

SERVES 4

4 sandwich-sized rolls or 1 (8-ounce) sweet baguette, cut into sandwich-sized rolls

1/4 cup extra virgin olive oil

1 tablespoon red wine vinegar

2 ounces arugula

4 roasted red bell peppers (page 215)

1 (7-ounce) can olive oil–packed imported Italian tuna

3 hard-boiled eggs, sliced

8 anchovy fillets (optional)

Slice the bread in half lengthwise. Pull out the doughy part of the bread to create a hollow, canoe-shaped shell with the crust. Drizzle the olive oil and vinegar over the inside of both halves of the rolls. Arrange the arugula over the bottom half of the rolls. Add a layer of peppers, tuna, and egg, and top with 2 anchovy fillets. Arrange the top of the bread over the ingredients and place a heavy skillet on the sandwich for 20 minutes to compress the ingredients and let the flavors meld. Cut each sandwich in half and serve.

Enjoy with Cakebread Cellars Rubaiyat or a light, fruity, slightly chilled red wine.

SUMMER

Prawn, Cherry Tomato, and Basil Pizza

A few years ago we remodeled our outdoor kitchen because we found that it was the perfect place to teach cooking classes in the summertime. We put in a wood-burning oven to anchor the eastern end of the kitchen and it is now in constant use because everything that emerges from it tastes so good. Pizzas are one of the most popular dishes cooked in it because they make a great hors d'oeuvre and guests can gather around the kitchen while they are being baked. The wood-burning oven's temperature rises much higher than an ordinary oven, so the pizzas cook in less than five minutes and have a very crisp, perfectly cooked crust. You can make pizzas on a grill if you don't have a wood-burning oven.

SERVES 6

6 pizza dough balls (page 213)

TOMATO SAUCE

2 tablespoons extra virgin olive oil

2 cloves garlic, minced

$1/4$ teaspoon crushed red pepper flakes

$1^1/2$ pounds ripe plum tomatoes, peeled, seeded, and diced

Kosher salt

TOPPING

2 tablespoons extra virgin olive oil plus additional for brushing

2 cloves garlic, minced

1 pound large prawns, peeled, deveined, and cut in half lengthwise

1 tablespoon chopped flat-leaf parsley

2 cups cherry tomatoes, halved

10 ounces grated provolone cheese

$1/4$ cup chopped fresh basil

Prepare the pizza dough as directed.

Preheat a wood-burning oven to medium heat, about 600°. (See page 213 for grill instructions.)

To make the tomato sauce: Combine the olive oil, garlic, and red pepper in a saucepan. Cook over medium heat for 1 minute. Add the tomatoes and a pinch of salt. Simmer for 15 to 20 minutes, until thick.

To prepare the topping: Heat the 2 tablespoons olive oil and garlic together in a large nonstick sauté pan over high heat. Add the prawns and parsley and cook for 2 to 3 minutes, until the prawns become opaque, stirring frequently. Set aside.

To assemble the pizzas: Stretch each ball of dough into an 8-inch circle or press the dough with your fingertips on a lightly floured surface to shape into a flat round about 8 inches in diameter. Spread 2 tablespoons of the tomato sauce on the top of each round and scatter a handful of prawns and tomato halves over this. Sprinkle with about $1/2$ cup of the cheese. Bake each pizza for 3 to 5 minutes, brushing the crust with olive oil occasionally. The pizza is ready when the cheese melts and the crust is brown and crispy. Sprinkle with the basil, cut into wedges, and serve.

Enjoy with Cakebread Cellars Sauvignon Blanc or a refreshing, light sauvignon blanc.

SUMMER

Tomato, Tapenade, and Fresh Herb Pizza

This pizza is a great showcase for sun-ripened tomatoes at the peak of their season. The tapenade offers a salty contrast to the sweet tomatoes—a perfect balance of wonderful flavors. It is delicious when it is pulled out of the oven and eaten immediately, but it tastes equally good slightly cooled, when the flavors have melded together. The tapenade can be made in advance and refrigerated in an airtight container for up to two weeks.

SERVES 6

6 pizza dough balls (page 213)

TAPENADE

2 cups kalamata olives, pitted

2 cloves garlic, minced

2 tablespoons capers, drained

$1/4$ cup extra virgin olive oil

TOPPING

6 ripe tomatoes, peeled and sliced

$1/2$ cup freshly grated Parmigiano-Reggiano

3 tablespoons chopped fresh oregano or marjoram

2 tablespoons extra virgin olive oil

$1/4$ cup chopped flat-leaf parsley

Prepare the pizza dough as directed.

Preheat a wood-burning oven to medium heat, about 600°. (See page 213 for grill instructions.)

To make the tapenade: Combine the olives, garlic, capers, and olive oil in a food processor. Process until a smooth paste is formed.

To assemble the pizzas: Stretch each ball of dough into an 8-inch circle or press the dough with your fingertips on a lightly floured surface to shape into a flat round about 8 inches in diameter. Spread about 1 tablespoon of the tapenade over each pizza round. Arrange a layer of tomato slices over the top and sprinkle with about 1 heaping tablespoon of the cheese. Sprinkle with even amounts of the oregano, drizzle the olive oil over the top, and bake for 3 to 5 minutes, until the crust is crisp and browned. Sprinkle with parsley, cut into wedges, and serve.

Enjoy with Cakebread Cellars Rubaiyat or a light-bodied, fruit-forward red wine that can be served chilled.

Roasted Garlic, Summer Squash, and Teleme Pizza

Subtle is the best way to describe this pizza. Each ingredient is mildly flavored, resulting in a refreshing food ideal for summer. The olive oil used for finishing should be the best available because its taste will be prevalent. The same is true for the pepper. If you don't have a pepper grinder, you can crack peppercorns with the side of a skillet, but store-bought ground black pepper should not be used.

SERVES 6

6 pizza dough balls (page 213)

$1/2$ cup roasted garlic purée (page 214)

2 small yellow and green summer squash, cut into paper-thin slices

3 tablespoons chopped fresh summer savory

8 ounces Teleme cheese, cut into slices

Extra virgin olive oil, for drizzling

Freshly ground black pepper

Medium-coarse sea salt

Prepare the pizza dough and the roasted garlic purée as directed.

Preheat a wood-burning oven to medium heat, about 600°. (See page 213 for grill instructions.)

Bring a large saucepan of salted water to a boil over high heat. Add the squash and cook for 30 seconds. Transfer to a colander and place under cold running water to stop the cooking process. Let drain completely.

Stretch each ball of dough into an 8-inch circle or press the dough with your fingertips on a lightly floured surface to shape into a flat round about 8 inches in diameter. Spread 1 heaping tablespoon of the roasted garlic purée over the top of each round. Arrange the squash over the top and sprinkle with the savory. Arrange the cheese over the squash and bake for 3 to 5 minutes, until the cheese is melted and the crust is crisp and browned. Drizzle the top with olive oil and sprinkle with black pepper and a pinch of sea salt. Cut into wedges to serve.

Enjoy with Cakebread Cellars Sauvignon Blanc or Rubaiyat, or a dry sauvignon blanc or light-bodied red wine that has a nice balance of fruit and acid.

🌸 SUMMER

Fish Tacos with Tropical Fruit Salsa

Available at Latin markets, achiote paste is a small, compacted block of ground annatto seed that has been seasoned with vinegar and herbs. It has an earthy taste not unlike a dried mild chile that lends an interesting flavor when used in marinades. Trivia buffs may be interested in knowing that the annatto seed is also used as a natural coloring agent for butter, margarine, and cheese.

SERVES 4 TO 6

1/3 cup fresh orange juice

1 tablespoon fresh lemon juice

2 tablespoons achiote paste

1 clove garlic, mashed to a paste

2 teaspoons chili powder

1/2 teaspoon kosher salt plus additional for seasoning

Cayenne pepper

1/4 cup extra virgin olive oil

2 pounds 1-inch-thick mahi mahi, sea bass, or albacore fillets, skinned

1 papaya (about 1 pound), diced

1/4 cup finely diced red onion

1 tablespoon minced cilantro

1 teaspoon seeded and finely minced serrano chile

1/4 teaspoon minced lime zest

2 tablespoons fresh lime juice

12 corn tortillas

2 cups finely shredded romaine lettuce

1 lime, cut into 6 wedges

In a large nonreactive bowl, whisk together the orange juice, lemon juice, achiote paste, garlic, chili powder, the 1/2 teaspoon salt, and a pinch of cayenne in a small bowl until thoroughly combined. Whisk in the olive oil. Put the fish in a shallow bowl or on a plate and pour the marinade over the fish. Let sit for 20 minutes.

Light and heat a charcoal grill to high heat.

Combine the papaya, onion, cilantro, serrano chile, lime zest, lime juice, and a pinch of salt in a small bowl. Stir to mix well. Set aside.

Put the fish on the grill and cook, uncovered, for 3 to 4 minutes per side, until firm and browned. Transfer to a bowl and break into large flakes.

Wrap the tortillas in aluminum foil and set on the grill over indirect heat. Cover and cook for 2 to 3 minutes, until heated through.

Arrange the tortillas on a flat surface and divide the fish among them. Top with a small handful of lettuce and a spoonful of the papaya salsa. Fold over the tortillas and serve with a lime wedge.

Enjoy with Cakebread Cellars Sauvignon Blanc or Rubaiyat, or a crisp, slightly chilled, dry sauvignon blanc or light-bodied red table wine.

SUMMER

Portobello Burger
with Grilled Onions and Aioli

One of Jack's favorites, this sandwich has all the flavor of an authentic burger but with an earthy, healthy appeal. Always check the mushrooms to be sure they are fresh. They should feel heavy and the tops and edges should be smooth. There shouldn't be any wrinkles or tears. Look at the underside to check that the gills are closed. Clean the mushrooms by wiping them with a dry paper towel or clean kitchen towel.

SERVES 6

6 portobello mushrooms, cleaned and stems trimmed

1 cup aioli (page 210)

$1/2$ cup extra virgin olive oil plus additional for brushing

Kosher salt

Freshly ground black pepper

2 small red onions, cut into 1-inch-thick slices

2 tablespoons balsamic vinegar

6 artisan-baked rolls (potato bread, sourdough, or sweet rolls), sliced lengthwise

6 leaves red or green leaf lettuce

Place the portobellos in a bowl with a damp paper towel over them to keep them moist.

Prepare the aioli as directed.

Light and heat a charcoal grill to high heat.

Arrange the mushrooms on a baking sheet. Brush with $1/4$ cup of the olive oil and sprinkle with salt and pepper.

Arrange the onion slices on a baking sheet and drizzle with the remaining $1/4$ cup olive oil and the vinegar. Sprinkle with salt and pepper.

Put the onions on the grill and cook for 2 minutes per side, until softened and brown grill marks appear. Transfer to the baking sheet.

Put the mushrooms top side up on the grill and cook for 2 to 3 minutes, until grill marks appear. Turn, brush the tops with olive oil, and cook for 3 to 4 minutes, until soft (you can test by squeezing them between tongs; if they bend easily they are done).

Set the rolls on the grill, cut side down, and cook for 2 to 3 minutes, until lightly toasted.

Spread equal amounts of the aioli on each roll. Arrange an onion slice, a mushroom, and a piece of lettuce on the bottom of each roll. Replace the tops, cut into quarters, and serve.

Enjoy with Cakebread Cellars Rubaiyat or a slightly chilled light wine with lots of red fruit flavors.

Pulled Pork Sandwich

Every year before our open house we gather to taste the wines we release and then Brian develops a dish to be paired with each wine. In 2002 he and Richard created these pulled pork sandwiches as bite-sized snacks to match our 1999 Cabernet Sauvignon. They were one of the most popular dishes served. This recipe requires a couple of days time because the pork needs to sit overnight to absorb the flavors of the rub and then it needs to be smoked for several hours. There may be leftover pork, but you'll be glad because it tastes just as great warmed up the next day as it does the first time you serve it. Be sure you have a big napkin nearby when you eat this. It's messy, but worth it.

SERVES 6

2 teaspoons sweet paprika

2 teaspoons chili powder

4 teaspoons kosher salt

2 teaspoons brown sugar

1 teaspoon ground cumin

1 teaspoon freshly ground black pepper

1/4 teaspoon cayenne pepper

1 (3-pound) pork butt

2 cups Richard's Cherry-Cola Barbecue Sauce (page 214)

1/2 head (1 pound) cabbage, quartered, cored, and shredded

1 carrot, peeled and grated

1/2 yellow onion, minced

1/2 cup mayonnaise

2 tablespoons apple cider vinegar

1 teaspoon celery seed

6 potato bread rolls

Combine the paprika, chili powder, 2 teaspoons of the salt, the brown sugar, cumin, black pepper, and cayenne pepper in a small bowl. Rub over the entire surface of the pork butt and refrigerate overnight.

Fire up a smoker or heat a charcoal grill to low, about 225°. Put the pork butt in the smoker. (If using a charcoal grill, add water-soaked wood chips to the barbecue before putting the pork butt on the grill.) Cook for 4 1/2 to 5 hours at a constant temperature of about 225°, until the meat pulls away from the bone and the internal temperature reaches 180°.

While the meat is smoking, prepare the barbecue sauce as directed.

Let the meat cool slightly. Remove the meat from the bone and chop or pull it into shreds. Transfer to a saucepan, add the barbecue sauce, and warm over medium-low heat while preparing the coleslaw.

Combine the cabbage, carrot, and onion in a colander. Sprinkle with the remaining 2 teaspoons of salt and let sit for 20 minutes. Squeeze to remove any excess liquid. Put in a bowl and add the mayonnaise, vinegar, and celery seed.

Slice the rolls in half and place a heaping spoonful of meat on the bottom of each roll. Top with a spoonful of the cabbage mixture. Set the top of the bread over the slaw and serve.

Enjoy with Cakebread Cellars Napa Valley Cabernet Sauvignon or a full-bodied red wine.

Herb Frittata, Arugula, and Roasted Pepper Panini

The trick to making this sandwich great is to tear out the doughy part of the bread rolls. All you are left with is the crisp crust cradling the savory egg mixture. Cook the eggs in a pan that is small enough for the eggs to reach the edges so you get an even thickness of egg. Although this is a sandwich, it is substantial and healthy enough to make a great dinner, and a quick dinner at that.

SERVES 4

8 large eggs

1/4 cup freshly grated Parmigiano-Reggiano

2 tablespoons chopped flat-leaf parsley

2 tablespoons chopped fresh basil

2 teaspoons chopped fresh sage

Kosher salt

Freshly ground black pepper

4 teaspoons unsalted butter

4 artisan-baked rolls (such as potato bread, herb, or sourdough)

1/4 cup extra virgin olive oil

1 tablespoon balsamic vinegar

2 ounces arugula

4 roasted red bell peppers (page 215)

Lightly beat the eggs with a whisk in a large bowl. Add the Parmigiano, parsley, basil, and sage. Add a pinch of salt and pepper. Heat a small nonstick skillet over high heat. Add 1 teaspoon of the butter and swirl it around in the pan to melt it. When it stops foaming, add one-quarter of the egg mixture and gently shake the pan for a few seconds to distribute the egg until the egg begins to set. Cook for 1 minute, until the egg is slightly firm and the bottom is lightly browned. Flip with a spatula and cook for 30 seconds to 1 minute, until browned. Transfer to a plate. Repeat with the remaining egg mixture to make 3 more frittatas.

Slice the rolls in half and drizzle with the olive oil and vinegar. Open up the peppers and lay them flat with an equal amount of arugula on the bottom of each roll. Cut each frittata in half and arrange both halves over the peppers. Place the top of the bread over the frittata, cut in half, and serve.

Enjoy with Cakebread Cellars Rubaiyat or Cabernet Sauvignon. These sandwiches are so versatile they can be enjoyed with red wines that range from light-bodied and fruity to full-bodied with dark fruit flavors, smooth tannins, and notes of black pepper and vanilla.

🦋 FALL

Dungeness Crab Melt

The challenge for our chefs every year when the time for open house arrives is to create dishes that are more substantial than an hors d'oeuvre but can still be eaten as finger food. Brian has mastered this and always creates a menu bursting with delicious treats. This crab melt has the comfort-food appeal of an old-fashioned tuna melt. This recipe, like all of the crab recipes at the winery, is made with Dungeness crab, but if Dungeness isn't available where you live, another lump crabmeat can be substituted.

SERVES 4 TO 6

$^1/_2$ pound Dungeness crabmeat, squeezed dry and picked through for shells

1 stalk celery, finely minced

$^1/_2$ small red onion, minced

$^1/_4$ cup mayonnaise

2 teaspoons Dijon mustard

1 teaspoon fresh lemon juice

1 teaspoon Old Bay Seasoning

1 teaspoon chopped fresh tarragon

$^1/_4$ teaspoon Worcestershire sauce

$^1/_4$ teaspoon Tabasco sauce

1 (1-pound) loaf artisan-baked rye bread, cut into $^1/_4$-inch-thick slices

4 ounces Swiss cheese, grated

4 to 6 gherkins, thinly sliced

Preheat the broiler.

Combine the crabmeat, celery, red onion, mayonnaise, mustard, lemon juice, Old Bay Seasoning, tarragon, Worcestershire, and Tabasco in a large bowl.

Arrange the bread on a baking sheet and set under the broiler, 1 to 2 minutes per side, until golden brown. Spread a small amount of the crabmeat mixture over each bread slice. Top with a spoonful of cheese and arrange on a baking sheet. Set under the broiler and cook for about 3 minutes, until the cheese melts and lightly browns. Garnish with a slice of gherkin and cut each sandwich in half. Serve warm.

Enjoy with Cakebread Cellars Napa Valley Chardonnay or a chardonnay with a silky mouthfeel and a lively, balanced fruit and acid.

Narsai David's Sweet Potato Bread

In 1988, our first restaurant customer and respected friend, Narsai David, joined us at the workshop. The following year he became the culinary director of the program and attended every year for nearly ten years. Of the many ways he made an impact on the workshop, one was the contribution he made every year when he baked his breads. The innovative loaves that he baked are the stuff of culinary legend. After the bread is baked, it benefits from sitting an hour or two before being sliced.

MAKES 2 LOAVES

3 tablespoons extra virgin olive oil

6 ounces sweet potato, peeled and cut into thick slices

1 cup water

1 cup millet seeds

2 tablespoons flax seeds

1 tablespoon nigella or caraway seeds

1 ($1/4$-ounce) package active dry yeast

$5^1/2$ cups bread flour

2 teaspoons kosher salt

Coat the bottom and sides of a bowl with 1 tablespoon of the olive oil. Line 2 baking sheets with parchment paper.

Put the potato in a small saucepan and cover with the water. Bring to a boil over medium heat, covered, and cook for about 10 minutes, until soft enough to mash easily. Remove from the heat and let cool in the water.

While the potato is cooking, combine the millet, flax, and nigella seeds in a small saucepan. Cook over medium heat for 3 to 4 minutes, until lightly toasted, stirring continuously to prevent burning. Transfer to a plate and let cool.

Transfer the potato with a slotted spoon to the bowl of a stand mixer or a large bowl. Pour the cooking water into a measuring cup, adding more water to reach a full 2 cups. When the water is cooled to room temperature (about 68°), add the yeast and stir to dissolve. Let sit for 5 to 10 minutes and then add to the potato.

Combine the flour, the remaining 2 tablespoons olive oil, and the salt in a separate bowl. Add to the sweet potato and yeast mixture and stir to distribute the dry ingredients. Mix with the dough hook if using a stand mixer, or with a wooden spoon, until the dough sticks together and forms a soft, springy mass. Knead for 5 minutes, until the dough is smooth. Add the seeds and knead until the seeds are evenly distributed in the dough. Place in the oiled bowl, cover loosely with plastic wrap, and set in a warm place. Let sit at room temperature for 1 to $1^1/2$ hours, until doubled in size.

Divide the dough into 2 portions and shape each into a ball. Set a ball in the center of each baking sheet. Dust lightly with flour and cover with a clean kitchen towel. Set in a warm place for 1 hour until doubled in size.

Preheat the oven to 400°. Cut slashes across the top of the bread in a tic-tac-toe pattern and set aside for 15 to 20 minutes while the oven is warming up.

Put the bread in the oven and spray the bottom of the oven with a water mister to create steam. Bake for 45 minutes, until golden brown, spraying with water every 10 or 15 minutes. Let sit at room temperature for 1 to 2 hours before slicing and serving.

WINTER

Pasta & Rice

Risotto with Asparagus, Prosciutto, and Lemon Zest

One of my favorite vegetables is asparagus. After the last spear is harvested for eating, the remaining stalks are left to go to seed to gain energy for the following year. Our asparagus plants grow ten feet tall and develop small red berries and fronds that look like wild fennel. This risotto appears to be very rich, but it is quite delicate and refreshing.

SERVES 4 TO 6

1/2 pound pencil-thin asparagus, cut into 1/2-inch pieces, tough ends discarded

2 tablespoons unsalted butter

1 small yellow onion, finely diced

1 ounce prosciutto, finely diced

1 cup carnaroli or arborio rice

6 cups warm chicken stock (page 212)

2 tablespoons dry white wine

1/3 cup freshly grated Parmigiano-Reggiano

1/4 teaspoon minced lemon zest

Kosher salt

Bring a large saucepan of salted water to a boil over high heat. Add the asparagus and cook for 1 minute, until al dente. Drain and rinse under cold running water.

Melt the butter in a large saucepan over medium-high heat. Add the onion and cook for 1 minute. Add the prosciutto and cook for 1 minute. Add the rice and cook, stirring, for 1 to 2 minutes, until the rice is coated with the butter. Add 1 cup of the stock and cook for about 3 minutes, until the liquid is absorbed, stirring constantly. Continue adding the stock 1 cup at time and stirring frequently. Cook for 15 to 20 minutes, until the rice becomes al dente and the mixture is creamy and moist. Stir in the asparagus and cook for 1 minute. Add the wine. Stir in the cheese and lemon zest. Let sit for 1 to 2 minutes. Season to taste with salt and serve.

Enjoy with Cakebread Cellars Napa Valley Chardonnay or a chardonnay with hints of green apple and pear flavors.

SPRING

Orecchiette with Leeks, Spring Peas, and Prosciutto

Peas are a spring crop that rely on the last little bit of cold to convert their starches to sugar. Unfortunately, the moment that peas are picked the sugar begins to convert back to starch, which makes them less sweet. For convenience, frozen peas can be used in this recipe.

SERVES 4 TO 6

3 small leeks, white parts only, finely diced (2$^{1}/_{2}$ cups)

2 tablespoons olive oil

2 turnips, peeled and cut into $^{1}/_{2}$-inch dice

2 cups frozen green peas

1 tablespoon chopped fresh mint

12 ounces dried orecchiette

2 ounces prosciutto, finely diced

$^{1}/_{2}$ cup finely grated Pecorino Romano

Kosher salt

Freshly ground black pepper

Put the leeks in a small bowl and cover with water. Let sit for about 5 minutes to let any sand or dirt settle to the bottom.

Heat the olive oil in a large saucepan over medium heat. Remove the leeks from the water and add to the pan. Add the turnips and cook for 7 to 10 minutes, until tender. Add the peas and mint and cook for 2 to 3 minutes.

While the vegetables are cooking, cook the pasta according to the package directions. Drain the pasta, reserving $^{1}/_{2}$ cup of the water.

Add the pasta to the vegetables. Stir in the prosciutto and Pecorino. Add the reserved water and toss to coat evenly. Season to taste with salt and pepper. Serve family style.

Enjoy with Cakebread Cellars Napa Valley Sauvignon Blanc or a dry, round, complex sauvignon blanc.

SPRING

Penne with Zucchini and Basil Sauce

This pasta dish is prepared in the same way that pasta alla carbonara, a classic Italian dish, is made, by adding the hot pasta to the sauce. The heat from the pasta gently cooks the egg, resulting in a creamy, rich sauce that coats the pasta and the zucchini.

SERVES 4 TO 6

1 pound zucchini, grated

Kosher salt

2 tablespoons extra virgin olive oil

3 large cloves garlic, chopped

2 eggs, beaten

1/4 cup finely grated Parmigiano-Reggiano

2 tablespoons finely grated Pecorino Romano

2 tablespoons chopped fresh basil

1 pound dried penne

Freshly ground black pepper

Put the zucchini in a large colander set over a sink or bowl. Sprinkle with salt and let sit for 20 minutes. Squeeze between your hands to eliminate any excess moisture.

Heat a large skillet over medium heat. Add the zucchini, olive oil, and garlic. Cook for 5 minutes, until softened. Remove from the heat and set aside.

In a large stainless steel bowl, combine the eggs, Parmigiano, Pecorino, and basil. Set aside.

Cook the pasta according to the package directions. Drain and add to the bowl with the eggs. Toss to coat. (The heat from the pasta will cook the eggs.) Add the zucchini and toss to combine. Season to taste with salt and pepper and serve.

Enjoy with Cakebread Cellars Chardonnay Reserve or a rich, full-bodied chardonnay.

Risotto with Sweet Corn, Chiles, and Squash Blossoms

There are two types of rice commonly used to prepare risotto: carnaroli and arborio. Both are a medium-grain rice with a high starch content that forms a creamy texture when cooked. Carnaroli cooks slightly faster and tends to be less gummy. It is the one we prefer. In this risotto, the rice is well-balanced by the delicate flavors of the other ingredients. It is light enough to be a first course or a side dish and delicious enough to be a full meal.

SERVES 4 TO 6

2 tablespoons unsalted butter

1 small yellow onion, finely diced

1 cup carnaroli or arborio rice

6 cups warm chicken stock (page 212)

1 cup fresh corn kernels (about 2 small ears)

5 Anaheim chiles, roasted, peeled, and diced

2 tablespoons dry white wine

6 squash blossoms, sliced ($1^{1}/_{2}$ loosely packed cups)

$^{1}/_{3}$ cup freshly grated Parmigiano-Reggiano

Kosher salt

Melt the butter in a large saucepan over medium-high heat. Add the onion and cook for 1 minute. Add the rice and cook for 1 minute, stirring, until the rice is coated with the butter. Add 1 cup of the stock and cook for about 3 minutes, until the liquid is absorbed, stirring constantly with a wooden spoon. Continue adding the stock 1 cup at a time and stirring continuously for 10 minutes. Add the corn. Cook for 5 to 10 minutes, adding stock as needed, until the rice becomes al dente. Stir in the chiles and wine and cook for 2 to 3 minutes. Add all but a small handful of the squash blossoms and the cheese. Stir to mix well. Season to taste with salt. Transfer to a warm serving bowl, garnish with the remaining squash blossoms, and serve.

Enjoy with Cakebread Cellars Napa Valley Chardonnay or a dry, silky chardonnay.

Michael Smith's Late Summer Zucchini Risotto with Basil Leaves and Crescenza

Michael Smith participated in our 2000 workshop along with his wife and chef-partner, Debbie Gold. Dynamic chefs with a clearly visible passion for food, they garnered the national spotlight during their tenure at Kansas City's American Restaurant, where they were in residence the year they came to our workshop. A culinary team to be reckoned with, they prepared dishes that demonstrated their straightforward yet innovative style. Michael prepared this risotto dish, which is creamy and decadent and still very fresh and summery.

SERVES 4 TO 6

7 tablespoons extra virgin olive oil

2 small, long green zucchini, peeled and thinly sliced

2 cups Sweet 100 tomatoes, peeled

1 teaspoon kosher salt plus additional for seasoning

1 yellow onion, finely diced

3 cloves garlic, minced

1 cup carnaroli or arborio rice

6 cups chicken stock (page 212)

1 Rond de Nice or medium-long zucchini, cut into $1/4$-inch dice

6 squash blossoms, julienned

$1/4$ cup Crescenza cheese

$1/4$ cup freshly grated Parmigiano-Reggiano

2 tablespoons chopped fresh basil

Heat 2 tablespoons of the olive oil in a small saucepan over medium heat. Add the sliced zucchini and cover. Reduce the heat to low and cook for 5 to 7 minutes, until soft. Transfer to a blender and purée while gradually adding 2 tablespoons of the olive oil to emulsify and thicken. Set aside.

Toss the tomatoes with 1 tablespoon of the olive oil and a pinch of salt and set aside.

Heat the remaining 2 tablespoons olive oil over high heat. Add the onion and the 1 teaspoon salt. Cook for 5 to 6 minutes, until the onion is soft. Add the garlic and cook for 1 minute. Add the rice and stir to coat evenly with the oil. Cook for 3 minutes, stirring constantly. Add 1 cup of the stock and cook for about 3 minutes, until the liquid is absorbed, stirring constantly. Continue adding the stock 1 cup at time and stirring frequently. Cook for 15 to 20 minutes, until the rice becomes al dente and the mixture is creamy and moist.

When the rice is finished, gently stir in the diced zucchini, squash blossoms, Crescenza, Parmigiano, basil, and half of the zucchini purée. Divide the risotto among the serving dishes and top with a dollop of the remaining purée and an equal distribution of the tomatoes.

Enjoy with Cakebread Cellars Napa Valley Chardonnay or a silky, fresh chardonnay with balanced fruit and acid.

❀ SUMMER

Paella with Pork, Linguiça, and Chicken

Traditional paella is cooked on the grill in a shallow pan. The ingredients are added in an order that suits the decreasing heat of the coals. This recipe can be prepared on the stove and finished in the oven, but the temperature will need to be adjusted frequently to mirror the gradually decreasing temperature of the grill. The ingredient portions are intended for a fourteen-inch paella pan, but can easily be modified to accommodate a different pan size by altering the amount of stock and rice. Just use a three-to-one ratio of stock to rice. The best type of rice to use is a medium-grain rice with a high starch content. Authentic paella is cooked with Bomba or Calasparra rice, but you can use arborio as a substitute.

SERVES 4 TO 6

1 cup aioli (optional, page 210)

4 to 6 tablespoons extra virgin olive oil

1 1/2 pounds pork shoulder, cut into 2-inch cubes

1/2 garlic bulb (cut in half crosswise)

8 cups chicken stock (page 212)

2 bay leaves

1/2 cup white wine

1 tablespoon sweet paprika (Spanish paprika is preferable)

1/2 teaspoon saffron threads

1 small (about 3 1/2 pounds) fryer chicken, cut into 10 pieces

2 small yellow onions, finely diced

1 1/2 pounds ripe tomatoes, peeled, seeded, and diced

2 cups medium-grain rice (such as Bomba, Calasparra, or arborio)

1 1/2 pounds linguiça sausage, halved lengthwise and cut into 2-inch lengths

1 (2-inch) sprig rosemary

1 teaspoon kosher salt

1 cup frozen peas

3 small red bell peppers, roasted, peeled, and cut into thin strips (page 215)

Prepare the aioli as directed.

Heat 2 tablespoons of the olive oil in a large, wide, high-sided pan over high heat. Add the pork and garlic and cook for 5 to 7 minutes, until evenly browned. Add the stock and bay leaves. Bring to a boil. Decrease the heat to low and cook on a low simmer for 1 1/2 hours.

While the pork is cooking, bring the wine to a boil in a small saucepan over high heat. Add the paprika and saffron. Remove from the heat and let steep for 20 minutes.

Light a charcoal fire or heat a gas grill to high heat.

Remove the garlic and bay leaves from the pork mixture and discard. Using a slotted spoon, transfer the pork to a bowl. Pour the stock into a 2-quart measuring cup. If the stock measures less than 6 cups, add enough water or chicken stock to bring it up to 6 cups.

Place the paella pan on the grill (see page 120 for alternative method) and heat until almost smoking. Add 2 tablespoons of the olive oil. When hot, add the chicken. Cook for 2 minutes per side, until browned. Transfer to a baking sheet. Carefully discard the oil if it looks burnt and replace with the remaining 2 tablespoons olive oil. Add the onions and cook for 3 to 4 minutes, until browned, stirring frequently. Add the tomatoes and cook for 5 minutes, until a thick paste forms. Add the rice, stir, and cook for 1 to 2 minutes,

(continued on page 120)

until it's well coated. Add the stock, paprika-wine mixture, pork, sausage, rosemary sprig, and salt. Add the dark chicken meat back to the pan, pushing it down into the rice. Cook for 10 minutes. Add the remaining chicken pieces and the peas, pushing them down into the rice. Arrange the peppers in a decorative fashion and cook for 10 minutes. Remove from the heat. Cover with a clean kitchen towel or aluminum foil and let steam for about 10 to 20 minutes, until the rice is completely tender. Serve warm with a dollop of aioli.

Note: The paella can be prepared in an ovenproof skillet. Preheat the oven to 350°. Start the paella as directed, over high heat. Continue cooking on high heat until the point when the tomato is added. Reduce the heat slightly and continue cooking and reducing the heat until the point when the dark chicken meat is added. Cook on a simmer over medium heat for 10 minutes. Add the remaining chicken and the peas and transfer the pan to the oven. Bake for 10 minutes. Remove from the oven. Cover with a clean kitchen towel and let steam for about 10 to 20 minutes, until the rice is completely tender.

Produce gardener Marcy Snow

Enjoy with Cakebread Cellars Merlot or Chardonnay Reserve. This is the kind of dish that tastes great with almost any type of wine that you put on the table.

SUMMER

Spinach Tortellini with Buttermilk Dressing and Shiitake Mushrooms

I began cooking this recipe years ago with tortellini I'd buy from Genova Deli in Oakland. Jack has always loved it and because it can be served at room temperature or cold it's convenient to make ahead of time and refrigerate. The tortellini has to be good quality, so I suggest buying it from a reputable Italian deli in your area. Sometimes I add fresh broccoli, prawns, or chicken and serve the dish as a main course. It makes a great lunch or dinner.

SERVES 4 TO 6

1 cup buttermilk

1/4 cup light cream cheese

3 cloves garlic, minced

1/4 teaspoon Tabasco sauce

Freshly ground black pepper

2 tablespoons extra virgin olive oil

2 shallots, minced

1/2 pound shiitake mushrooms, stemmed and sliced

1/4 cup chardonnay or dry white wine

1 tablespoon fresh lemon juice

4 tablespoons chopped flat-leaf parsley

1 pound spinach tortellini

Put the buttermilk, cream cheese, 1 of the garlic cloves, the Tabasco, and a pinch of pepper in the blender. Process until smooth. Set aside.

Heat the olive oil in a large sauté pan over medium-high heat. Add the shallots and the remaining 2 garlic cloves. Cook for 2 to 3 minutes, until translucent and soft, but not brown. Add the mushrooms and cook for 8 to 10 minutes, until tender. Add the wine, lemon juice, and 2 tablespoons of the parsley.

While the mushrooms are cooking, prepare the tortellini according to the package directions. Transfer to a colander to drain. Put in a serving bowl and immediately add one quarter of the buttermilk mixture. Stir to coat evenly and allow to cool until the sauce begins to thicken. Arrange in pasta bowls and top with equal amounts of the mushroom mixture and the remaining buttermilk mixture. Sprinkle with the remaining 2 tablespoons parsley. Let cool to room temperature and serve.

Enjoy with Cakebread Cellars Napa Valley Chardonnay or a chardonnay that is dry, crisp, and fresh tasting.

SUMMER

Risotto with Escarole, Cremini Mushrooms, and Fontina

Escarole is a member of the versatile endive family. It has a slightly bitter taste when consumed raw in salads, which dissipates when it's cooked. The inner, pale yellow-green leaves are the most tender and tasty, so discard the tough, darker leaves.

SERVES 4 TO 6

2 tablespoons unsalted butter

1 small yellow onion, finely diced

1 cup carnaroli or arborio rice

6 cups warm chicken stock (page 212)

$1/2$ pound cremini mushrooms, cleaned and sliced

2 cups chopped escarole

4 ounces fontina, grated

Kosher salt

Truffle oil (optional)

Melt the butter in a large saucepan over medium-high heat. Add the onion and cook for 1 minute. Add the rice and cook for 2 to 3 minutes, until the rice is coated, stirring constantly with a wooden spoon. Add 1 cup of the stock and cook for about 3 minutes, until the liquid is absorbed, stirring constantly. Continue adding the stock 1 cup at time and stirring frequently. Cook for 10 minutes. Add the mushrooms and escarole and cook for 5 minutes, until the rice becomes al dente and the mixture is creamy and moist. Stir in the cheese. Season to taste with salt. Transfer to a serving bowl and drizzle with a few drops of truffle oil.

Enjoy with Cakebread Cellars Napa Valley Chardonnay or Chardonnay Reserve, or a silky, dry, fruit-forward chardonnay.

Acini di Pepe with Manila Clams and Turnip Greens

If you like pasta with clams, you will really enjoy this pasta. Acini di pepe are very small pieces of pasta that soak up the flavors of the clams and their juices and pack a lot of taste. If you prefer, you can substitute Swiss chard for the turnip greens.

SERVES 4 TO 6

2 bunches turnip greens, cut into thirds

$1/3$ cup white wine

2 pounds Manila clams, soaked and scrubbed

1 pound dried acini di pepe

2 tablespoons extra virgin olive oil

3 anchovy fillets, chopped

4 cloves garlic, chopped

Kosher salt

Freshly ground black pepper

Bring a large pot of salted water to a boil. Add the turnip greens and cook for 1 to 2 minutes, until wilted. Transfer to a colander with a slotted spoon, reserving the cooking water. Place under cold running water to stop the cooking process. Squeeze between your hands to remove any excess liquid. Transfer to a cutting board and chop into a fine mixture. Set aside.

Bring the wine to a boil in a large, high-sided skillet over high heat. Add the clams, cover, and cook for about 5 minutes, until the clams open. Transfer the clams and their juices to a bowl to cool.

Return the water from the greens to a boil. Add the pasta and cook according to the package directions.

While the pasta is cooking, rinse the skillet and return to high heat. Add the olive oil, anchovies, and garlic. Cook for 1 to 2 minutes. Add the greens and cook for 1 to 2 minutes, until hot. Drain the pasta and add to the skillet with the greens. Stir in the clams and their juices. Season to taste with salt and pepper and serve.

Enjoy with Cakebread Cellars Napa Valley Chardonnay or a crisp, fruity, dry chardonnay.

🌸 FALL

Rigatoni with Lamb and Rosemary Sauce

This pasta is ideal for tucking into on a cold night when you have a roaring fire going and want a rustic, hearty dish. It does require some attention, but the effort and the time spent cooking are well worth it.

SERVES 4 TO 6

2 tablespoons extra virgin olive oil

1 small yellow onion, finely minced (1 cup)

1 small carrot, peeled and finely minced (1 cup)

1 large stalk celery, finely minced (1 cup)

1 pound ground lamb

1 tablespoon tomato paste

3 cloves garlic, minced

$1/2$ teaspoon chopped fresh rosemary

$1^1/2$ cups dry red wine (such as syrah)

1 (28-ounce) can whole tomatoes, drained, squeezed to remove seeds and juices, and chopped, juices reserved

6 cups lamb or chicken stock (page 212)

Kosher salt

Freshly ground black pepper

12 ounces red or green chard, stems removed

1 pound dried rigatoni

$1/2$ cup freshly grated Parmigiano-Reggiano

Heat the olive oil over medium heat. Add the onion, carrot, and celery and cook for 5 minutes, until soft, stirring occasionally. Add the lamb and cook for about 10 minutes, until the meat is nicely browned and the bottom of the pan becomes coated with a brown glaze. Add the tomato paste, garlic, and rosemary and cook for 1 to 2 minutes, until the garlic becomes aromatic. Add the wine, tomatoes, and reserved tomato juices. Cook, partially covered, for 30 minutes, until almost dry. Add 2 cups of the stock and decrease the heat to low. Cook, partially covered, on a low simmer for 30 minutes, until the mixture becomes thick. Add another 2 cups of the stock and cook, partially covered, for 30 minutes, until the mixture thickens again. Add the remaining 2 cups stock and cook, partially covered, for 30 to 45 minutes, until thick. Season to taste with salt and pepper.

While the sauce is cooking, heat a large saucepan over high heat. Add the chard and cook for 1 to 2 minutes, until the leaves are completely wilted. Stir to cook evenly. Transfer to a colander to drain. Place under cold running water and then squeeze with your hands to remove any excess liquid. Transfer to a cutting board and chop finely.

Cook the pasta according to the package directions.

While the pasta is cooking, add the chard to the sauce and cook for 5 minutes. Drain the pasta in a colander. Add the pasta and cheese to the sauce. Toss to mix. Season to taste with salt and pepper. Serve family style or in individual bowls.

Enjoy with Cakebread Cellars Syrah or a smooth, dry syrah with blackberry, licorice, and dark chocolate flavors balanced by just the right amount of acid.

🌺 WINTER

Spaghettini with Crab, Tomato, and White Wine

When the crab, which is fairly fragile, is added to the pasta it has a tendency to break apart. Don't despair. The flavors disperse and you get a little bit of crab in every bite. Gently combining the two will help preserve some of the large lumps of crabmeat.

SERVES 4 TO 6

2 tablespoons extra virgin olive oil

3 cloves garlic, minced

2 tablespoons chopped flat-leaf parsley plus additional for garnish

$^1/_4$ teaspoon crushed red pepper flakes

$2^1/_2$ pounds ripe plum tomatoes, peeled, seeded, and diced

$^1/_2$ cup dry white wine (such as sauvignon blanc)

12 ounces dried spaghettini

1 pound crabmeat, picked over for shells and squeezed to remove any excess liquid

Kosher salt

Freshly ground black pepper

Heat the olive oil, garlic, the 2 tablespoons parsley, and the crushed red pepper together in a large, wide-bottom saucepan. Cook for 1 to 2 minutes, until the garlic is soft. Add the tomatoes and wine. Cook for 7 to 10 minutes, until reduced by one-quarter. Season with a pinch of salt and pepper.

While the sauce is cooking, cook the pasta according to the package directions.

Drain the pasta in a colander and add to the tomato mixture. Toss to coat the pasta. Add the crab and toss gently, being careful not to break up the crab too much. Divide among serving bowls and sprinkle with parsley to garnish.

Enjoy with Cakebread Cellars Sauvignon Blanc or Napa Valley Chardonnay. We have an affinity for crab with crisp, fruity chardonnay, but in this pasta, the tomatoes add a spark that really suits a dry, light-bodied sauvignon blanc.

WINTER

Seafood & Shellfish

Pan-Roasted Halibut with Orange, Sherry, and River Ranch Honey

A few years ago, we decided to put honeybees in our River Ranch garden to take advantage of the fruit, flora, and fauna that surround the small farmhouse there. We had Spencer Marshall put in one of his hives and we've been harvesting the best honey ever since. Spencer and his wife have over 650 hives around the Bay Area, from which they gather and sell regional honey. Our honey is especially delicious with the delicate flavors of halibut and it balances the sherry we use, which is Amontillado, a sherry with a nutty flavor characteristic. Like cooking with wine, using a high-quality sherry will result in a better dish.

SERVES 4

1 cup Amontillado or dry sherry

1 cup fresh orange juice

2 teaspoons honey

4 tablespoons extra virgin olive oil

1 to 2 teaspoons fresh lemon juice

4 (5- to 6-ounce) halibut fillets, skinned

Kosher salt

Freshly ground black pepper

1 teaspoon chopped fresh chives

Bring the sherry to a rapid boil in a small saucepan set over high heat. Cook for 3 to 4 minutes, until reduced by half. Add the orange juice and honey and cook for 10 to 12 minutes, until the liquid becomes thick and is reduced to $1/2$ cup. Whisk in 2 tablespoons of the olive oil. Taste for sweetness and if too sweet, adjust the taste with the lemon juice

Heat a large nonstick skillet over high heat. Add the remaining 2 tablespoons olive oil to the skillet. Season the halibut with salt and pepper and add to the pan. Cook for 4 to 5 minutes per side, until browned. Transfer to a warm serving dish, spoon the sauce over the fish, and sprinkle the chives over the top.

Enjoy with Cakebread Cellars Napa Valley Chardonnay or a fresh, fruity, dry chardonnay.

SPRING

Sturgeon with Celery Root, Peas, and Oyster Mushrooms with Spring Pea Sauce

Sturgeon is a dense, meaty fish. Thicker fillets usually need to be finished in the oven to ensure that they are thoroughly cooked. The celery root, mushrooms, and peas are a perfect match for it, especially when it is served with Celery Root Purée (page 174). At first glance it may seem like this recipe has a lot of steps, but the result is an elegant dish in both taste and presentation.

SERVES 4

SAUCE

2 tablespoons butter

2 shallots, minced

1 cup chicken stock (page 212)

1 cup frozen green peas

VEGETABLES

2 tablespoons extra virgin olive oil

1 large (about 10 ounces) celery root, peeled and cut into $1/2$-inch cubes

4 ounces oyster mushrooms

2 shallots, minced

1 cup frozen peas

1 tablespoon chopped flat-leaf parsley

FISH

2 tablespoons extra virgin olive oil

4 (6-ounce) sturgeon fillets, skinned

Kosher salt

Freshly ground black pepper

Preheat the oven to 400°.

To make the sauce: Melt the butter in a small skillet over medium heat. Add the shallots and cook for 4 to 5 minutes, until softened. Add the stock and bring to a boil. Add the peas and cook for 1 to 2 minutes. Transfer to a blender. Put the lid on the blender and remove the vent cover on the top. Cover the vent with a towel to release steam. Purée. Wipe out the saucepan and strain the sauce through a fine-mesh sieve into the saucepan. Set aside.

To make the vegetables: Heat the olive oil in a small nonstick skillet. Add the celery root and cook for 2 to 3 minutes, until slightly browned. Add the mushrooms and shallots and cook for 3 to 4 minutes, until the mushrooms begin to brown, stirring to distribute the heat evenly. Add the peas and parsley and cook for 1 to 2 minutes.

To make the fish: Heat a large ovenproof sauté pan over high heat. Add the olive oil. Season the fish with salt and pepper and cook for 2 to 3 minutes per side, until golden brown. Transfer to the oven and bake for 5 minutes, until firm and cooked through.

While the fish is baking, warm the pea sauce over medium heat. Spoon the sauce into the center of 4 warm serving plates. Arrange a spoonful of the vegetable mixture on the pea sauce and top with a piece of fish.

Enjoy with Cakebread Cellars Napa Valley Chardonnay or Chardonnay Reserve, or a luscious chardonnay with oak nuances.

✿ SPRING

❧
American Harvest Workshop Recipe

Walter Pisano's Pan-Roasted Sturgeon with Manila Clams and Buttered Leeks

In 1999, Walter Pisano came to our workshop from Seattle, where he has been courting the food cognoscenti at Tulio for many years. His rustic yet refined Italian cuisine was a departure from his classical French training, but it was obviously his forte as he has continued to attract glowing reviews for his cooking. This sturgeon dish combines the elegance of French cuisine with his love of Italian minimalism and fresh, local ingredients.

SERVES 4

4 (4- to 6-ounce) sturgeon fillets, skinned

1 teaspoon minced fresh rosemary

1 teaspoon kosher salt

1 pound leeks, white parts only, cut into 2-inch lengths, halved, and cut into $1/2$-inch strips lengthwise

4 tablespoons extra virgin olive oil

3 cloves garlic, sliced

$1^1/2$ pounds clams

1 cup dry white wine

1 cup chicken stock (page 212)

Pinch of crushed red pepper flakes

1 tablespoon chopped flat-leaf parsley

2 tablespoons unsalted butter

Rub the sturgeon with the rosemary and salt and refrigerate for 30 minutes.

Preheat the oven to 400°.

Put the leeks in a bowl and cover with water. Let sit for about 5 minutes to let any sand or dirt settle to the bottom.

Heat 2 tablespoons of the olive oil and the garlic in a skillet over high heat. Add the clams, wine, stock, and crushed red pepper. Cover and cook for 2 to 3 minutes, until the clams begin to open, shaking the pan every few minutes. Transfer to a colander set over a bowl. Remove the clams from the shells, setting aside 8 unshelled clams. Strain the liquid through a fine-mesh sieve into a small saucepan. Add the shelled clams and parsley. Keep warm over low heat.

Remove the leeks from the bowl of water with your hands and transfer to a colander to drain. Melt the butter in a sauté pan over medium heat. Add the leeks and cook for about 5 minutes, until tender, stirring constantly to prevent burning. Set aside.

Heat a large ovenproof skillet over high heat. Add the remaining 2 tablespoons olive oil. Add the sturgeon and cook for 2 minutes per side, until browned. Transfer to the oven and bake for 5 to 6 minutes. Place a spoonful of the leeks in the center of 4 warm serving bowls. Set a piece of fish in the center of each and spoon the broth from the clams over the top. Top each with 2 unshelled clams and serve.

Enjoy with Cakebread Cellars Napa Valley Chardonnay or a rich chardonnay with depth and concentrated fruit flavors.

❧ SPRING

Grilled King Salmon
with Roasted Tomato Vinaigrette

A hardwood charcoal such as mesquite, which is what we use, is the best choice for grilling the salmon in this recipe because it imparts a pleasant smokiness. Be sure to place the salmon on the grill skin side down. A good indication that the fish is cooked is when a spatula will slide easily between the fish and the skin. If the skin sticks to the grill, just remove the fish from the skin. This tomato vinaigrette sets off the smoky flavors well. We use tomatoes picked and roasted at the end of summer, when the tomato vines are heavy with fruit, because the flavors become concentrated and make a versatile ingredient.

SERVES 4 TO 6

1 clove garlic, cut into thin slivers

1 1/2 pounds ripe plum tomatoes, halved lengthwise

3/4 to 1 cup extra virgin olive oil plus additional for brushing

1 teaspoon fresh thyme leaves

Kosher salt

Freshly ground black pepper

1/4 cup champagne vinegar

1 shallot, minced

1 (2-pound) king salmon fillet, with skin

Preheat the oven to 400°.

Push a garlic sliver into the flesh of each tomato half. Arrange cut side up on a baking sheet and drizzle with 1/4 cup of the olive oil. Sprinkle the thyme and salt and pepper over the tomatoes. Bake for 1 1/2 to 2 hours, until the skin begins to pull away from the flesh and the tomatoes become soft and shriveled. Once or twice while baking, tilt the pan to collect the oil in the corner and spoon over the tomatoes. Let cool.

Light and heat a charcoal grill to medium heat.

Combine the vinegar, shallot, and a pinch of salt and pepper in a bowl. Let sit for 20 minutes.

Peel and chop 4 of the tomatoes; reserve the rest for garnish. Pour any oil remaining in the baking sheet into a large measuring cup and add enough olive oil to reach 3/4 cup. Add the chopped tomatoes to the vinegar mixture. Whisk in the olive oil in a slow, steady stream.

Brush the salmon with olive oil, sprinkle with salt and pepper, and place on the grill skin side down. Cover and cook for 10 to 15 minutes, until cooked through. Remove the salmon from the grill with a metal spatula. Don't worry if the fish separates from the skin, just scrape the skin off later. Transfer to a serving dish and drizzle with the vinaigrette.

Enjoy with Cakebread Cellars Chardonnay Reserve or a chardonnay with toasty oak, vanilla, and mineral characteristics.

Sea Scallops with Sweet Corn, Roasted Peppers, and Shiitake Mushrooms

Scallops are incredibly easy to prepare, and they cook in no time at all. The trick to cooking them properly is to heat the pan to a very high heat and then add the scallops to sear them on the outside. Once they become brown, which should happen within a minute or two, they can be removed from the heat. This way they finish cooking from the residual heat and won't become overcooked.

SERVES 4

3 tablespoons unsalted butter

2^1/$_2$ cups fresh corn kernels (3 to 4 ears)

1 celery stalk, minced (^{1}/$_2$ cup)

2 green onions, minced (^{1}/$_2$ cup)

^{1}/$_2$ pound shiitake mushrooms, sliced

3 red bell peppers, roasted, peeled, and diced (page 215)

1 tablespoon chopped parsley

Kosher salt

Freshly ground black pepper

2 tablespoons extra virgin olive oil

1 pound sea scallops

Melt the butter in a large skillet over medium heat. Add the corn, celery, and green onions. Cook for 1 to 2 minutes, until the corn softens. Add the mushrooms and peppers. Cook for 8 to 10 minutes, until the mushrooms begin to turn crisp, stirring occasionally. Add the parsley and stir to mix. Season with a pinch of salt and pepper. Transfer to a serving platter.

Heat the olive oil in a large sauté pan over high heat. Season the scallops with salt and pepper and add to the skillet. Cook for 2 minutes, until evenly browned. Turn and cook the other side for 1 minute. Arrange over the vegetables and serve.

Enjoy with Cakebread Cellars Napa Valley Chardonnay or Chardonnay Reserve, or a fruity, full-bodied chardonnay with oak, citrus, and vanilla nuances.

SUMMER

Cedar-Plank Salmon with Richard's Cherry-Cola Barbecue Sauce

Richard Haake, our southern chef who owned a barbecue restaurant in Georgia, introduced us to the recipe for this sauce during our 2002 open house. The sweetness of the cola plays with the heat from the paprika and chipotle, giving it a great balance of flavors that complement a wide variety of meat and seafood, from pork to salmon. The salmon in this recipe is cooked on a piece of cedar wood that is set directly on the grill. Cedar planks can be purchased at a lumber store and should be untreated, at least two inches thick, and soaked overnight in water before each use. The salmon is cooked with the indirect heat and smoke that are trapped by the lid, so the color changes very little but the fish cooks all the way through and the result is a satiny texture.

SERVES 6

1/2 cup Richard's Cherry-Cola Barbecue Sauce (page 214)

6 (4- to 6-ounce) salmon fillets or 1 whole filleted side of salmon, skinned

Resident chef Richard Haake

Soak a 2- by 8-inch-long cedar plank in water overnight.

Prepare the barbecue sauce as directed.

Light and heat a charcoal grill to high heat. When the coals are white-hot, put the plank on the center of the grill for 5 minutes, until the wood begins to smoke.

Arrange the salmon directly on the plank, brush with the sauce, cover, and cook for 15 to 20 minutes, until firm to the touch and dark brown. Transfer to a serving dish and serve with any remaining sauce on the side.

Enjoy with Cakebread Cellars Pinot Noir or a pinot noir with allspice, cloves, and pretty red fruit characteristics.

🌿 SUMMER

Grilled Fish Brochettes with Charmoula and Harissa

Wahoo is a firm white Hawaiian fish that is also called *ono*. It has a rich, dense flavor that benefits from being cooked over mesquite. In this recipe, the fish is rubbed with charmoula, a savory spice mixture, and served with harissa on the side. These brochettes are wonderful served over Couscous with Currants and Toasted Almonds (page 180).

SERVES 4 TO 6

1/2 cup charmoula (page 211)

1/4 cup harissa (page 213)

2 pounds firm white fish (such as wahoo, albacore, or swordfish), cut into 1-inch cubes

12 five-inch wooden skewers

1/4 cup loosely packed cilantro leaves, for garnish

Prepare the charmoula and the harissa as directed.

Put the fish in a bowl and add the charmoula. Toss to coat well. Refrigerate for 1 hour.

Soak the skewers in water for 20 minutes.

Light and heat a charcoal grill to high heat.

Thread each skewer with 4 pieces of fish. Place on the grill and cook for 5 to 6 minutes, until lightly charred, turning to cook all sides evenly. Transfer to a serving platter and sprinkle with the cilantro. Serve a small bowl of harissa on the side.

Enjoy with Cakebread Cellars Sauvignon Blanc or Rubaiyat, or a dry, fruity, and thirst-quenching sauvignon blanc or light red wine.

Fennel-Crusted Ahi with Garden Herb Salad

The salad part of this recipe really pays tribute to the herbs in our garden. Almost every type of herb we grow is included, as well as the leaves from the delicate celery stalks in the heart of the bunch. Brian often adds these leaves to salads because they provide a subtle celery taste. The tuna, which is seared and then chilled before being served, should be the best quality you can find. If you can, buy sushi-grade pieces and slice the fish into steaks at home.

SERVES 4 TO 6

$1/2$ cup aioli (page 210)

1 small fennel bulb, outer leaves removed, halved, cored, and cut into paper-thin slices, fronds reserved

$1/2$ cup fennel fronds

4 radishes, cut into paper-thin slices

1 cup loosely packed assorted torn basil

1 cup flat-leaf parsley

$1/2$ cup yellow celery leaves (from the heart)

$1/2$ cup tarragon leaves

2 tablespoons chopped fresh chives

$1/4$ cup crushed fennel seed

Kosher salt

Freshly ground black pepper

2 (8-ounce, 2-inch-thick) ahi tuna fillets

4 tablespoons extra virgin olive oil

1 tablespoon fresh lemon juice

Prepare the aioli as directed.

Combine the fennel, fennel fronds, radishes, basil, parsley, celery leaves, tarragon, and chives in a large bowl. Set aside.

Sprinkle the fennel seeds, salt, and pepper over both sides of the tuna. Heat a large skillet over high heat. Add 2 tablespoons of the olive oil. Add the tuna and cook for $1^1/2$ minutes on each side, until slightly browned. Transfer to a plate and refrigerate.

Pour the remaining 2 tablespoons olive oil and the lemon juice over the salad and toss to coat well. Season to taste with salt and pepper.

Cut the tuna into $1/2$-inch-thick slices and arrange a few slices on each of 4 plates. Drizzle with the aioli and top with equal amounts of the salad.

Enjoy with Cakebread Cellars Chardonnay Reserve or Rubaiyat, or a dry chardonnay with pineapple, lemon, and melon flavors. A light, dry, fruity red wine that can be served chilled makes a good choice as well.

SUMMER

— 137 —

Alaskan Halibut with Warm Herb Vinaigrette

Our garden includes a profusion of fresh herbs, which are incorporated into nearly every dish cooked here at the winery. The heat of this warm vinaigrette showcases the flavors of the herbs. They need to be added at the last minute to retain and present their color. If you grow herbs, you will appreciate dishes like this, which make good use of your plants; like flowers, herbs need to be deadheaded in order to allow new growth.

SERVES 4

2 tablespoons champagne vinegar

1 shallot, minced

$1/2$ cup plus 2 tablespoons extra virgin olive oil

4 (6-ounce) halibut fillets, skinned

Kosher salt

Freshly ground black pepper

1 tablespoon chopped flat-leaf parsley

1 teaspoon chopped fresh tarragon

1 teaspoon chopped fresh chives

1 teaspoon chopped fresh thyme

Combine the vinegar and shallot in a small saucepan. Let sit for 20 minutes. Whisk in the $1/2$ cup olive oil in a slow, steady stream. Set aside.

Heat a large sauté pan over high heat. Add the 2 tablespoons olive oil. Season the fish with salt and pepper and cook for 4 to 5 minutes per side, until golden brown.

While the fish is cooking, heat the vinaigrette over medium-low heat to warm it through.

Divide the fish among 4 warm plates. Add the parsley, tarragon, chives, and thyme to the vinaigrette and spoon over each piece of fish.

Enjoy with Cakebread Cellars Napa Valley Chardonnay or Chardonnay Reserve, or a dry, silky chardonnay with balanced fruit, acid, and oak.

SUMMER

Grilled Mahi Mahi with Pumpkin Seed Salsa

Tomatillos look like green tomatoes wrapped in a thin papery husk. Though, like the tomato, they are a member of the nightshade family, they have a tart flavor and a firm texture that's similar to a bell pepper. They can be eaten raw, but roasting them softens the skin and adds complexity to their taste. In this recipe the traditional Mexican technique is used in which the tomatillos are added to a dry pan and cooked over high heat until the skins begin to blister. Serve the mahi mahi with Wilted Cabbage Slaw with Chorizo (page 181).

SERVES 4

1 pound tomatillos, peeled

1 large jalapeño

3 cloves garlic, unpeeled

1 cup loosely packed cilantro leaves

$1/4$ cup toasted pumpkin seeds (page 214)

$1/4$ cup fresh orange juice

2 tablespoons extra virgin olive oil

1 tablespoon fresh lime juice

$1/4$ teaspoon ground cumin

4 (6-ounce) mahi mahi fillets, skinned

Kosher salt

Freshly ground black pepper

Heat a large skillet over medium heat. Add the tomatillos, jalapeño, and 2 of the garlic cloves. Cook for about 10 minutes, until the skin on the vegetables begins to blacken and blister. Transfer to a cutting board. Cut the jalapeño in half and remove and discard the seeds and stems. Put in a blender. Peel the garlic and add to the blender. Add the tomatillos, cilantro, and pumpkin seeds. Purée. Set aside.

Light and heat a charcoal grill to high heat.

Combine the orange juice, olive oil, lime juice, and cumin in a small bowl. Peel and chop the remaining garlic clove. Add to the orange juice mixture. Put the fish in a shallow pan and pour the orange juice mixture over the top. Let sit for 20 minutes, turning once or twice to distribute the marinade.

Moisten a kitchen towel with olive oil and carefully rub the grill. Repeat 2 to 3 times to create a coating on the grill to prevent the fish from sticking. Season the fish with salt and pepper and place on the grill at a slight angle. Cook, uncovered, for 1 to 2 minutes. Shift the fish to an angle in the opposite direction to create hatch marks and cook for 1 to 2 minutes. Turn the fish and cook the other side for 1 to 2 minutes. Transfer to a serving platter and top with a spoonful of salsa.

Enjoy with Cakebread Cellars Sauvignon Blanc or Rubaiyat, or a crisp, light, dry sauvignon blanc or slightly chilled red wine.

FALL

Prawns with Tomato, Feta, and Oregano

Inspired by the classic Greek dish *sagenaki,* this prawn dish is appealing on many levels. It is very pretty; there is a pleasing contrast in texture between the prawns, the tomatoes, and the feta; and the crushed red peppers give it a zippy taste. The feta cheese we like is made by Skyhill Farms, which is owned by Amy Wend, who has been making goat cheeses since 1989. She has participated in our American Harvest Workshop for many years, introducing chefs to her fresh goat cheeses. Serve these prawns with lots of crusty French bread to soak up the juices.

SERVES 4

2 tablespoons extra virgin olive oil

2 cloves garlic, minced

Pinch of crushed red pepper flakes

1 pound large prawns, peeled and deveined, with tails on

1 pound ripe plum tomatoes, peeled, seeded, and diced

$1/2$ cup dry white wine (such as chardonnay)

$1/2$ teaspoon dried oregano

Kosher salt

Freshly ground black pepper

$3/4$ cup crumbled feta cheese

2 tablespoons flat-leaf parsley

Preheat the oven to 500°.

Heat a large skillet over high heat. Add the olive oil, garlic, and crushed red pepper. Cook for 1 minute. Add the prawns and cook for 2 to 3 minutes, until the prawns turn pink. Add the tomatoes, wine, and oregano. Cook for 1 to 2 minutes. Season with a pinch of salt and a few grinds of pepper. Transfer to a shallow casserole dish. Sprinkle the cheese and parsley over the top and bake for 5 minutes, until the cheese melts. Serve immediately.

Enjoy with Cakebread Cellars Napa Valley Chardonnay or a dry chardonnay with fresh fruit flavors and a silky texture.

FALL

Sicilian-Style Swordfish Steaks Stuffed with Pine Nuts, Currants, and Saffron

This is a popular Sicilian dish that most likely was influenced by the numerous cultures, including Arabs, Moors, and Greeks, that roamed the Mediterranean island for centuries. Saffron, which is grown in Italy's Sardegna and Abruzzo regions, is a popular spice used liberally in southern Italy. In Sicily, this dish is often prepared with the entire tail of a swordfish, but it tastes just as good with steaks, which are easier to prepare.

SERVES 6

1/4 cup currants

1/4 cup plus 2 tablespoons extra virgin olive oil

1/2 cup minced yellow onion

Pinch of saffron threads

1 cup dry bread crumbs (page 215)

1/4 cup pine nuts, toasted and chopped

1/4 teaspoon fennel seeds, chopped

6 (6-ounce, 1/2-inch-thick) swordfish steaks

Kosher salt

Freshly ground black pepper

Put the currants in a small bowl and cover with hot water. Let sit for 20 minutes until soft and plump. Drain.

Heat the 2 tablespoons olive oil in a large skillet over medium heat. Add the onion and saffron and cook for 10 minutes, until the onion is soft, but not browned. Transfer to a bowl. Add the currants, 1/2 cup of the bread crumbs, the pine nuts, and fennel seeds and stir to combine.

Make a cut with a sharp boning or paring knife in the center of each swordfish steak and cut along the entire length to form a pocket. Place 1/4 cup of the onion mixture in the center of each steak. Secure the closure with a toothpick. Brush both sides of each steak with the 1/4 cup olive oil and sprinkle with salt and pepper. Coat both sides lightly with the remaining 1/2 cup bread crumbs. Pour any remaining olive oil into a large skillet and heat over high heat. Add the swordfish and cook for 2 to 3 minutes per side, until lightly browned and cooked through. Remove the toothpicks and serve.

Enjoy with Cakebread Cellars Napa Valley Chardonnay or a dry, crisp chardonnay.

FALL

— 141 —

Prawns Stuffed with Garlic-Toasted Bread Crumbs

Jack calls these robustly flavorful prawns a healthy man's fried calamari. The prawns are stuffed with bread crumbs and cooked and eaten in their shells, which makes them very crunchy and delicious. They can be served as a main course, but they also make a great hors d'oeuvre.

SERVES 4 TO 6

1 pound (about 24) medium prawns, unpeeled, tails on

1/2 cup dry bread crumbs (page 215)

2 small cloves garlic, minced

1 tablespoon chopped fresh parsley

1/4 teaspoon kosher salt

4 tablespoons extra virgin olive oil

1 lemon, cut into wedges

Using a serrated knife, make a cut lengthwise down the back of the prawns, through the shell but not the tail, deveining the prawns as you go.

Mix the bread crumbs, garlic, parsley, and salt in a small bowl. Add 2 tablespoons of the olive oil and mix with your hands to evenly distribute the oil. Stuff each prawn with 1 teaspoon of the bread crumb mixture, firmly packing it into the entire length of the prawn.

Heat a large nonstick skillet over high heat. Add the remaining 2 tablespoons olive oil and the prawns. Cook for about 5 minutes, until bright orange, stirring to cook evenly. Serve warm with the lemon wedges.

Enjoy with Cakebread Cellars Napa Valley Chardonnay or a chardonnay with a silky texture and lots of fruit flavors.

WINTER

– 142 –

Crab Cakes

Nancy Oakes, the chef and owner of Boulevard in San Francisco, created a crab cake recipe for us the year she attended our American Harvest Workshop. They were unforgettable. Inspired by Nancy, Brian created this recipe, which uses fresh bread crumbs to keep the cakes moist. He also uses a lot of crab because that's what crab cakes should taste like; the other ingredients should provide a subtle background. The egg whites help to keep the cakes airy instead of too dense.

SERVES 4 TO 6

1 pound crabmeat, picked over for shells and squeezed to remove any excess liquid

$1^{1}/_{2}$ cups fresh bread crumbs (page 215)

1 stalk celery, finely minced ($^{1}/_{2}$ cup)

1 green onion, finely minced ($^{1}/_{4}$ cup)

$^{1}/_{4}$ cup mayonnaise

1 tablespoon fresh lemon juice

1 tablespoon chopped flat-leaf parsley

2 teaspoons Dijon mustard

1 teaspoon Worcestershire

1 teaspoon Tabasco sauce

2 eggs, separated

Extra virgin olive oil

1 lemon, cut into wedges

Combine the crabmeat, bread crumbs, celery, green onion, mayonnaise, lemon juice, parsley, mustard, Worcestershire, Tabasco, and egg yolks in a large bowl. In a separate bowl, whisk the egg whites until stiff peaks form. Fold the egg whites into the crab mixture. Shape $^{1}/_{3}$ cup of the crab mixture into a 2-inch-wide patty. Repeat with the rest of the mixture.

Add enough olive oil to fill a large nonstick skillet $^{1}/_{4}$-inch deep. Heat over medium-high heat. Add the crab cakes, in a single layer, and cook for 3 to 4 minutes per side, until golden brown. Arrange on a serving platter and serve with the lemon wedges.

Enjoy with Cakebread Cellars Napa Valley Chardonnay or a silky chardonnay with a good balance of fruit and acid.

WINTER

Meat & Poultry

Spring Lamb Stew with New Potatoes and Fava Beans

This is the last stew we make before the chill of early spring gives way to warmer days. It is the best of all worlds: a comforting one-dish meal made with the ingredients eagerly anticipated all winter. We often serve meals family style at the winery and this stew is perfect for that. Pour it into a decorative bowl or tureen and then pass it around the table.

SERVES 6

1/4 cup extra virgin olive oil

3 1/2 pounds lamb stew meat, trimmed

2 ounces pancetta, minced

2 cloves garlic, minced

1 teaspoon minced fresh rosemary

1/8 teaspoon crushed red pepper flakes

2 pounds ripe plum tomatoes, peeled, seeded, and chopped

3/4 cup white wine

1 1/2 pounds new potatoes

1 teaspoon kosher salt plus additional for seasoning

3 1/2 pounds fava beans, shelled

Freshly ground black pepper

Heat a large Dutch oven over high heat. Add the olive oil and let heat until almost smoking. Add the lamb in two or three batches to cook it uncrowded in a single layer. Cook for about 10 minutes, until evenly browned. Transfer the lamb to a plate once it is finished cooking. When all of the lamb is finished cooking, add the pancetta, garlic, rosemary, and crushed red pepper to the pot. Cook for 1 to 2 minutes, until softened. Add the tomatoes and wine and cook for 2 minutes. Add the lamb, decrease the heat to low, and cook on a low simmer for 1 1/2 hours, until the meat is tender.

While the lamb is cooking, put the potatoes in a saucepan and cover with cold water. Add the 1 teaspoon salt and bring to a boil over high heat. Reduce the heat and cook on a simmer for 15 minutes, until tender when pierced with a fork. Drain. Cut into quarters.

Bring a large pot of salted water to a boil. Add the fava beans and cook for 30 seconds to 1 minute, depending on the size and freshness of the beans, until tender. Transfer to a colander to drain and place under cold running water to stop the cooking process. Remove the thin skin on each bean.

When the meat is tender, add the potatoes and cook, partially covered, for 20 minutes. Add the fava beans and cook, uncovered, for 5 minutes. Season to taste with salt and pepper. Serve family style or in individual bowls.

Enjoy with Cakebread Cellars Napa Valley Cabernet Sauvignon or a velvety cabernet sauvignon with dark fruit, smooth tannins, and hints of spice, cedar, and pepper.

Pan-Roasted Chicken Breasts with Roasted Garlic and Spinach

Recipes are only as good as the ingredients that are used to prepare them. Chicken dishes benefit by beginning with a high-quality bird. We prefer to use organically raised, free-range chickens that are locally grown. Seeking out growers in your area is worth the time, and trying different types side by side will give you the best means of comparison. Pan roasting chicken is a foolproof method for ensuring juicy meat.

SERVES 4

1 tablespoon roasted garlic purée (page 214)

2 tablespoons extra virgin olive oil

2 cloves garlic, sliced

1 teaspoon chopped fresh thyme

4 boneless chicken breasts

Kosher salt

Freshly ground black pepper

1 bunch spinach, stemmed and washed

$^1/_4$ cup dry sherry

$^3/_4$ cup brown chicken stock (page 210)

Prepare the roasted garlic purée as directed.

Combine the olive oil, garlic, and thyme in a small bowl. Spread over the chicken, season with salt and pepper, and refrigerate for 4 hours or overnight.

Preheat the oven to 450°.

Heat a large nonreactive, ovenproof skillet over high heat. Add the chicken skin side down and cook for 2 to 3 minutes per side, until golden brown. Transfer to the oven and bake for 5 to 7 minutes, until cooked through.

While the chicken is baking, heat a large skillet over high heat. Add the spinach in batches and cook for 1 to 2 minutes, until wilted, stirring to cook evenly. Transfer to a colander to drain. Rinse under cold running water. Squeeze gently between your hands to eliminate any excess water.

Transfer the chicken to a warm plate. Return the skillet to the stovetop and add the sherry. Cook on high heat for 2 to 3 minutes, until the sherry is almost entirely evaporated. Add the stock and garlic purée and whisk to fully incorporate the garlic. Cook for 2 to 3 minutes, until the sauce begins to thicken slightly, whisking often. Add any chicken juices that have collected on the plate. Add the spinach and cook for 30 seconds. Transfer the spinach to a warm serving platter using tongs or a slotted spoon. Top with the chicken and spoon the sauce over the top. Serve immediately.

Enjoy with Cakebread Cellars Napa Valley Chardonnay or a dry, crisp chardonnay with a silky texture.

American Harvest Workshop Recipe

Frank Stitt's Herb-Marinated Rack of Lamb with Niçoise Olives

Frank Stitt has the heart of a southerner and the soul of a Frenchman. This was reflected in every dish he prepared at the 1999 workshop, including this savory lamb dish that makes use of only a few ingredients—his signature flair. His restaurant in Birmingham, Alabama, Highlands Bar & Grill, is the stage for stunning dishes that showcase the southern ingredients he was raised eating, the global skills he honed while studying and cooking with such culinary giants as Alice Waters and Richard Olney, and a food sensibility that is all his own.

SERVES 4 TO 6

5 tablespoons extra virgin olive oil

3 cloves garlic, smashed

2 teaspoons minced fresh rosemary

2 teaspoons minced fresh oregano

2 teaspoons minced fresh thyme

2 teaspoons minced flat-leaf parsley

2 racks (about 1½ pounds each) lamb, trimmed

10 cloves garlic, peeled

½ cup dry red wine (such as cabernet sauvignon or merlot)

1 cup brown chicken stock (page 210)

½ cup peeled, seeded, and diced tomato

¼ cup pitted niçoise olives

Combine 2 tablespoons of the olive oil, the smashed garlic, the rosemary, oregano, thyme, and parsley in a small bowl. Set the lamb in a shallow dish and rub the herb mixture evenly over the racks. Refrigerate for at least 4 hours or overnight.

Preheat the oven to 400°. Put the peeled garlic cloves on a small sheet of aluminum foil. Add 1 tablespoon of the olive oil and toss to coat evenly. Fold the edges of the foil together to create a sealed package. Set on a baking sheet and bake for 20 to 30 minutes, until soft. Set aside.

Heat an ovenproof skillet over high heat. Add the remaining 2 tablespoons olive oil. Add the lamb and cook for 2 minutes per side, until browned on both sides. Transfer to the oven and bake for about 12 minutes for medium-rare. Transfer the lamb to a plate and return to the oven to keep warm. Add the wine to the skillet and cook over high heat for 2 to 3 minutes, until the wine is almost entirely evaporated, stirring to loosen any stuck bits of meat from the sides and bottom of the pan. Add the stock and bring to a boil. Cook for 3 to 4 minutes, until reduced by half. Add the tomatoes, olives, and roasted garlic and cook for 1 to 2 minutes. Cut the lamb into individual chops, arrange on serving dishes, and spoon the sauce over the lamb.

Enjoy with Cakebread Cellars Napa Valley Cabernet Sauvignon or Merlot, or a full-bodied, velvety cabernet sauvignon or merlot that expresses vanilla, berry, and black pepper flavors.

SUMMER

Baby Back Ribs with Red Wine Vinegar, Rosemary, and Sweet Peppers

Ribs are a flavorful cut of meat that stand up to long cooking times. In this dish they are cooked until the meat almost falls off the bone. The rosemary and peppers provide a rustic, earthy background. Serve the ribs with Classic Mashed Potatoes (page 188) or Traditional Soft Polenta (page 185).

SERVES 4 TO 6

2 tablespoons extra virgin olive oil

1$^1/_2$ sides (about 4 pounds) baby back ribs, cut into 2- to 3-rib portions

Kosher salt

Freshly ground black pepper

3 cloves garlic, cut into slivers

2 pounds ripe plum tomatoes, peeled, seeded, and diced

$^1/_2$ cup red wine vinegar

2 sprigs rosemary

2 teaspoons sugar

3 sweet red bell peppers, seeded and cut into $^1/_2$-inch-thick strips

Heat the olive oil in a large high-sided skillet. Season the ribs with salt and pepper and add to the skillet. Cook for 3 to 4 minutes on the meat side, until evenly browned. Transfer the meat to a plate. Add the garlic to the pan and cook for 1 minute. Add the tomatoes, vinegar, rosemary, and sugar. Cook for 1 to 2 minutes. Return the meat to the pan and arrange in a single layer. Cover and cook over low heat for 1 hour.

Add the peppers, stir the contents to mix, cover partially, and cook for 30 minutes, until the peppers are tender. Remove the ribs from the pot and increase the heat to high. Cook for 10 to 15 minutes, until the liquid is reduced to a thick sauce. Return the ribs to the pan. Heat through and serve over mashed potatoes or soft polenta.

Enjoy with Cakebread Cellars Merlot or a merlot that is full-bodied and complex with fruit-forward flavors. We like merlot because it stands up to the peppers.

SUMMER

Leg of Lamb with Green Olive–Almond Tapenade and Tomato Jam

Don and Carolyn Watson are niche farmers who raise lambs in Calistoga, in the northern part of Napa Valley. Their locally grown lamb is the best we've ever tasted and we are so pleased to include them every year in our American Harvest Workshop. Don brings a whole lamb and lets the chefs select the cuts they want to use. This recipe uses the leg, which you can buy and butterfly yourself, or ask the butcher to remove the bone for you. At a glance, the tapenade and tomato jam require several ingredients, but most are common pantry items and both recipes can be made ahead and refrigerated for up to one week.

SERVES 4 TO 6

LAMB

$^1/_2$ cup charmoula (page 211)

1 (3$^1/_2$-pound) leg of lamb, butterflied

TAPENADE

2 cups pitted large green olives

$^1/_2$ cup whole almonds

1 tablespoon chopped cilantro

1 tablespoon chopped flat-leaf parsley

1 clove garlic, chopped

$^1/_2$ cup extra virgin olive oil

1 tablespoon fresh lemon juice

TOMATO JAM

2 tablespoons extra virgin olive oil

2 cloves garlic, chopped

3 pounds ripe plum tomatoes, peeled, seeded, and coarsely chopped

2 teaspoons sweet paprika

1 teaspoon cumin seeds, toasted and ground

1 teaspoon coriander seeds, toasted and ground

1 teaspoon kosher salt

$^1/_4$ teaspoon cayenne pepper

1 tablespoon chopped cilantro

1 teaspoon honey

$^1/_4$ teaspoon ground cinnamon

1 teaspoon sesame seeds, toasted

To make the lamb: Prepare the charmoula as directed. Rub over the entire surface of the lamb to coat evenly. Refrigerate for 2 hours.

To make the tapenade: Combine the olives, almonds, cilantro, parsley, and garlic in a food processor. Pulse to combine. Add the olive oil with the motor running. Process until a smooth paste forms. Add the lemon juice and pulse to combine. Transfer to a serving bowl.

To make the tomato jam: Heat a large skillet over high heat. Add the olive oil and garlic and cook for 2 minutes, until the garlic softens. Add the tomatoes, paprika, cumin, coriander, salt, and cayenne pepper. Cook for 20 to 30 minutes, stirring often, until a thick paste forms. Add the cilantro, honey, and cinnamon. Cook for 5 minutes, until the flavors meld. Transfer to a serving bowl and let cool to room temperature. Top with a sprinkle of sesame seeds.

Light and heat a charcoal grill to high heat.

Put the lamb on the grill and cook for 12 to 15 minutes for medium-rare, until both sides are darkened and the meat feels firm to the touch. Baste occasionally with the marinade. Transfer to a cutting board and let sit for 5 minutes. Cut against the grain into thick slices, arrange on a warm serving platter, and serve with the tapenade and the jam.

Enjoy with Cakebread Cellars Napa Valley Cabernet Sauvignon or a cabernet that has a balance of fruit and acid with cedar, spice, licorice, and vanilla characteristics.

Cakebread Vineyard's Howell Mountain Ranch

Pan-Roasted Chicken Breasts
with Cherry Tomatoes, Basil, and Garlic

Cherry tomatoes, which are as delicious hot as they are cold, grow in almost any conditions and can be planted in containers or in the ground. Only a few plants are needed to yield a small assortment. Using a variety of tomatoes in this chicken dish will result in a mixture of flavors and a very attractive presentation. Serve with Traditional Soft Polenta (page 185) or Classic Mashed Potatoes (page 188).

SERVES 4

2 tablespoons extra virgin olive oil

4 boneless chicken breasts

Kosher salt

Freshly ground black pepper

2 cloves garlic, minced

1 pound ripe plum tomatoes, peeled, seeded,
    and chopped (1 cup)

$1/2$ cup white wine

2 cups assorted cherry tomatoes

2 tablespoons chopped fresh basil

Preheat the oven to 450°.

Heat a large nonreactive, ovenproof skillet over medium-high heat. Add the olive oil. Season the chicken with salt and pepper and place it skin side down in the skillet. Cook for 3 to 4 minutes per side, until evenly browned and nearly cooked through. Transfer to a plate. Add the garlic to the skillet and cook for 1 minute, until softened. Add the tomatoes and wine and cook for 2 to 3 minutes, until thickened. Stir to combine. Return the chicken to the skillet and bake uncovered in the oven for about 5 minutes, until cooked through. Return to the stove, add the cherry tomatoes and basil, and cook on high heat for 2 to 3 minutes, until the tomatoes begin to soften. Spoon some of the tomatoes and sauce from the pan into the center of each plate and top with a chicken breast.

Enjoy with Cakebread Cellars Napa Valley Chardonnay or Pinot Noir, or a chardonnay or pinot noir that is fruit-forward, crisp, and dry.

SUMMER

Dolores's Rolled Chicken

I cooked this chicken dish at one of the first formal lunches we held for the press. We served it with our zinfandel and one of our guests, Margaret Mallory, then the food editor of the *Oakland Tribune,* liked it so much that she devoted an entire page to the recipe and to me. For years we served it with our zinfandel because the fruitiness of the wine was a nice complement to the salty taste of the ham and salami. We stopped making our zinfandel in 1994, but we hope to have it back again, especially to enjoy with this dish, which Jack and I like cold. I usually refrigerate it for about four hours after it's baked.

SERVES 4 TO 6

1 (3- to 3^1/$_2$-pound) whole fryer chicken, deboned, with skin

^{1}/$_3$ cup dry bread crumbs (page 215)

^{1}/$_4$ cup chopped flat-leaf parsley

1^1/$_2$ teaspoons dried oregano

Kosher salt

Freshly ground black pepper

^{1}/$_4$ pound thinly sliced baked ham

10 oil-cured black olives, pitted and diced

^{1}/$_3$ pound thinly sliced Genoa salami

3 whole hard-boiled eggs, peeled

^{1}/$_2$ pound applewood-smoked bacon

Preheat the oven to 350°.

Spread a piece of plastic wrap or waxed paper on a flat surface and arrange the chicken in the center, skin side down. Place a second piece of plastic wrap over the chicken and pound with the bottom of a heavy saucepan or a mallet to flatten the chicken.

Combine the bread crumbs, parsley, and 1 teaspoon of the oregano in a small bowl.

Remove the top piece of plastic wrap from the chicken and sprinkle the chicken with salt and pepper. Arrange the ham slices over the entire surface of the chicken. Spread the bread crumb mixture over the top of the ham. Spread the olives over the bread crumbs and arrange the salami slices over the entire surface. Place the eggs in a line in the center, lengthwise. Pick up one long side of the chicken and fold over the eggs. Roll the chicken to form a long cylinder. Secure in 3 to 4 places with kitchen twine. Sprinkle with the remaining ^{1}/$_2$ teaspoon oregano and season with salt and pepper.

Put on a baking sheet and lay the bacon slices over the roll, crosswise, until the entire chicken roll is covered. Bake for 50 minutes, until the bacon is crisp, basting occasionally with the oil and juices that collect in the baking sheet. Remove the bacon and reserve for another use. Increase the oven temperature to 450° and bake for 10 to 15 minutes, until the roll is lightly browned.

Transfer to a cutting board. Let cool completely before slicing and serving.

Enjoy with Cakebread Cellars Rubaiyat or another dry, fruity red wine, such as pinot noir or zinfandel.

SUMMER

Filet Mignon with Grapes, Watercress, and Blue Cheese

Recently, we've made the acquaintance of the Giacomini family, who make a superb blue cheese that is one of the best in the United States. Their cheese, Point Reyes Blue, is robust, creamy, piquant, and great as part of a cheese course or as an ingredient. Sprinkled over the top of the filet, it complements the savory beef and slightly tart grapes in this recipe, bringing the recipe into balance.

SERVES 4

2 tablespoons grapeseed or vegetable oil

1 tablespoon unsalted butter

4 (6-ounce) filet mignon steaks

Kosher salt

Freshly ground black pepper

1 cup red seedless grapes

3/4 cup red wine

2 tablespoons balsamic vinegar

4 ounces watercress leaves

1 head Belgian endive, coarsely chopped

2 ounces blue cheese

Heat a stainless steel skillet over high heat. Add the oil and butter and cook until the butter stops foaming. Season the steaks with salt and pepper and add to the skillet. Cook for 1 to 2 minutes per side, until the steaks are seared. Transfer the steaks to a warm plate. Discard the oil from the skillet. Add the grapes to the skillet and cook for 1 minute over high heat. Add the wine and vinegar and cook for 1 to 2 minutes, until reduced to a light sauce. Pour any juices that have collected from the meat into the pan. Cook for 1 to 2 minutes.

Combine the watercress and endive in a small bowl. Divide among 4 plates. Place a steak slightly off center over each stack of greens. Spoon some grapes around the plate and crumble equal amounts of the blue cheese over the top of the meat. Spoon the sauce from the pan over the steak and greens and serve.

Enjoy with Cakebread Cellars Napa Valley Cabernet Sauvignon or a masculine cabernet sauvignon with bright fruit and smooth tannins.

FALL

❧

Alan Wong's Five-Spice Grilled Quail with Truffle Yaki Sauce

Alan Wong came to our fourth workshp in 1990, from Hawaii, where he was the chef at the Mauna Lani Bay Hotel. He traveled here again in 1996 when we celebrated the workshop's tenth anniversary. Alan was in good company that year, when many of the workshop alumni returned to measure the strides American cuisine had taken since the workshop's inception. Alan, who was born in Tokyo and raised in Hawaii, learned to cook on the Islands before heading to the Greenbriar in West Virginia and then Lutèce in New York City. He returned to Hawaii to open Alan Wong's Restaurant. His multicultural heritage inspires his signature cuisine, which blends Eastern ingredients with Western techniques, resulting in dishes like this quail, which he grilled for our guests and his culinary peers.

SERVES 4 TO 6

3 tablespoons water

2 tablespoons soy sauce

2 tablespoons grapeseed oil

2 tablespoons rice vinegar

2 tablespoons fresh lime juice

1 tablespoon mirin

1 tablespoon sugar

$^{1}/_{4}$ teaspoon sesame oil

1 clove garlic, smashed

3 ($^{1}/_{4}$-inch-thick) slices peeled fresh ginger

2 teaspoons cornstarch

$^{1}/_{2}$ cup heavy whipping cream

1 teaspoon white truffle oil

6 semi-boneless quail

Kosher salt

Freshly ground black pepper

Light and heat a charcoal grill to high heat.

Whisk together 2 tablespoons of the water, the soy sauce, grapeseed oil, vinegar, lime juice, and mirin in a bowl. Stir in the sugar, sesame oil, garlic, and ginger. Let sit for 20 minutes.

Transfer the soy sauce mixture to a small saucepan. Bring to a boil over high heat. Stir the remaining 1 tablespoon water and cornstarch together in a small bowl until the cornstarch dissolves. Whisk into the soy sauce mixture and cook for 1 to 2 minutes, until thickened. Gradually whisk in the cream and remove from the heat. Whisk in the truffle oil.

Season the quail with salt and pepper and place on the grill. Cook for 2 to 3 minutes per side, until evenly browned. Arrange on a serving platter and spoon the cream sauce over the quail.

Enjoy with Cakebread Cellars Pinot Noir or Chardonnay Reserve, or a silky, medium-bodied red or white wine with lots of fruit flavors and hints of toasted oak.

❧ FALL

Pork Chops with
Mushroom-Caper Pan Sauce

When Brian cooks a meat dish that requires transferring the meat to a plate while the pan is used for a sauce, he sets a bowl upside down on a plate and leans the meat against it. The juices collect in the plate but the meat isn't lying in them and they are easier to add back to the pan to make the sauce. We use thick pork chops for this recipe because they stay juicier.

SERVES 4 TO 6

4 (1^1/$_2$-inch-thick) boneless pork loin chops

Kosher salt

Freshly ground black pepper

1 tablespoon unsalted butter

2 tablespoons extra virgin olive oil

^{3}/$_4$ pound cremini mushrooms, wiped clean

1 cup dry sherry

1^1/$_2$ cups brown chicken stock (page 210)

3 sprigs thyme

2 tablespoons capers, drained

Preheat the oven to 450°.

Season the pork chops with salt and pepper on both sides. Combine the butter and olive oil in an oven-proof skillet large enough to hold the pork in a single layer. Heat over high heat. Add the pork chops and cook for 2 to 3 minutes per side, until browned. Transfer the pork chops to the oven, reserving the butter and olive oil mixture. Bake the pork chops for 10 minutes, until cooked nearly all the way through. Transfer the chops to a plate.

Return the pan with the butter and olive oil to the stove and heat over high heat. Slice the mushrooms ^{1}/$_4$ inch thick, add to the pan, and cook for 1 to 2 minutes, until soft. Add the sherry and cook for 4 to 5 minutes at a rapid boil, until the liquid evaporates. Add the stock and thyme and cook for 8 to 10 minutes, until the liquid is reduced by half. Add the capers and any juices from the pork chops that have collected on the plate and cook for 1 to 2 minutes. Remove the thyme sprig from the sauce before serving. Arrange the pork chops on 4 warm plates. Spoon the sauce over the pork chops and serve.

Enjoy with Cakebread Cellars Chardonnay Reserve or a luscious chardonnay with tropical fruit flavors and vanilla and oak characteristics.

FALL

Chicken under a Brick

The weight of a brick set on top of a chicken pushes out the fat from the chicken and cooks the outside to an otherwise unattainable crisp texture. Frankly, it does make a mess, but there simply isn't any other way to cook a chicken that will result in the same juicy meat and ultra crispy exterior. The chicken needs to be refrigerated for two hours before it is cooked to absorb the flavors of the olive oil, pepper, and lemon.

SERVES 4 TO 6

1 small (about 3^1/$_2$ to 4 pounds) fryer chicken

^{1}/$_4$ cup extra virgin olive oil

2 tablespoons fresh lemon juice

2 tablespoons cracked black pepper

2 teaspoons kosher salt

Remove the backbone from the chicken with a heavy knife or poultry shears. Pull the wings back and fold under the first joint. Make an incision between the breast and thigh and slide the leg joint through it to make the chicken sit flat. Arrange on a sheet of parchment in a baking dish. Rub both sides of the chicken with the olive oil, lemon juice, peppercorns, and salt to coat evenly. Refrigerate for 2 hours for the flavors to meld.

Wrap a large, heavy brick with aluminum foil. Remove the chicken from the refrigerator and let sit at room temperature for 20 minutes.

Heat a large cast iron skillet over medium heat. Add the chicken skin side up and put the brick on top of the chicken. Cook for 12 to 14 minutes, until the skin is crispy and darkly browned. Remove the brick, turn the chicken, and replace the brick. Cook for 15 to 20 minutes, until the skin is crispy and browned and the meat is cooked through. Cut into pieces and serve.

Enjoy with Cakebread Cellars Rubaiyat or Chardonnay Reserve, or a slightly chilled, fruity, dry red wine or a chardonnay with concentrated fruit and citrus characteristics.

FALL

Liberty Duck Breast with Dried Cranberry—Apple Bread Salad

This recipe was adapted from a dish that Debbie Gold created when she participated in our 2000 American Harvest Workshop. It is made with duck breasts from Sonoma County Poultry, which is owned by Jim Reichardt, a purveyor with whom we have enjoyed a wonderful relationship for a long time. A third-generation duck farmer, Jim left the family business to grow his own ducks in Penngrove, a small town on the eastern side of Sonoma County. There, he raises his liberty ducks exclusively for chefs and gourmet food markets.

SERVES 4 TO 6

4 (6- to 8-ounce) boneless Liberty or Peking duck breasts

2 cups dry red wine

$1/2$ cup dried cranberries

$1/2$ cup plus 1 tablespoon extra virgin olive oil

4 cups crustless sweet French bread cubes

$1/2$ cup pecans, toasted and chopped

1 tablespoon chopped flat-leaf parsley

1 teaspoon fresh thyme

Kosher salt

Freshly ground black pepper

$1^1/2$ pippin or Braeburn apples, peeled, cored,
    and diced (2 cups)

$1/2$ cup brown chicken stock (page 210)

Trim the duck breasts, score the skin, and set aside.

Combine the wine and cranberries in a medium saucepan and bring to a boil over medium-high heat. Remove from the heat and let sit for 20 minutes, until the berries are plump and moist.

While the berries are sitting, heat the $1/2$ cup olive oil in a large nonstick saucepan over high heat. Add the bread and toss to coat evenly with the oil. Cook for 5 minutes, until lightly browned on all sides, tossing occasionally to prevent burning. Transfer to a large bowl.

Drain the cranberries over a small saucepan to catch the wine. Set the cranberries aside. Return the wine to a boil over high heat. Cook for 10 to 15 minutes, until reduced to about $1/4$ cup.

Add the cranberries, pecans, parsley, and thyme to the bowl with the bread.

Season the duck with salt and pepper. Heat the 1 tablespoon olive oil in a large sauté pan over high heat. Add the duck, skin side down, reduce the heat to medium, and cook for 6 to 7 minutes, until golden brown. Turn and cook the other side for 3 to 4 minutes, until firm. Transfer the duck to a plate, drain all but 2 tablespoons of the fat from the pan, and return to high heat. Add the apples and cook for 3 to 5 minutes, until soft and golden brown. Add to the bread mixture.

Return the skillet to high heat and add the stock. Pour any duck juices that collect on the plate into the skillet. Bring to a boil and scrape the sides and bottom with a wooden spoon to loosen any stuck bits of duck or apple. Cook on a rapid simmer for 2 to 3 minutes, until thick. Add to the bread salad and toss to mix well. Season to taste with salt and pepper.

Cut the duck breasts into thin slices. Place a spoonful of the bread salad on the center of the plate. Arrange the sliced duck over the bread salad, spoon a small amount of the reduced wine around the plate, and serve.

Enjoy with Cakebread Cellars Benchland Select or Pinot Noir, or a full-bodied red wine with lots of ripe red fruit flavors.

🦋 FALL

Roast Pork Loin with Apple Brandy and Whole-Grain Mustard Sauce

At a glance, this recipe calls for a time commitment. The pork is infused with flavor from garlic, sage, and bay leaves that are wrapped around it, so it has to marinate for at least four hours. Fortunately, it can marinate overnight and the actual cooking time is relatively short.

SERVES 4 TO 6

1 (3^1/$_2$-pound) center-cut boneless pork loin

3 cloves garlic, cut in slivers

1 tablespoon chopped fresh sage

2 teaspoons cracked black pepper

2 teaspoons kosher salt

2 bay leaves, crumbled

2 tablespoons extra virgin olive oil

^{1}/$_2$ large yellow onion, chopped

1 large carrot, peeled and chopped

1 large stalk celery, chopped

2 to 3 pork bones

^{1}/$_2$ cup apple brandy or Calvados

1^1/$_2$ cups brown chicken stock (page 210)

1 tablespoon whole-grain mustard

Set the pork loin on a piece of plastic wrap and sprinkle all sides with the garlic, sage, pepper, salt, and bay leaves. Wrap tightly in the plastic wrap and refrigerate for at least 4 hours and up to 24 hours.

Preheat the oven to 450°.

Heat a large ovenproof skillet over high heat. Add the olive oil. Wipe off the herbs and garlic from the pork and add to the skillet. Cook for 1 to 2 minutes, until browned. Turn the pork and add the onion, carrot, celery, and pork bones to the pan. Cook for 2 to 3 minutes, until the meat and vegetables are lightly browned. Bake for 30 minutes, until the roast feels firm to the touch and the internal temperature reaches 145°, turning a few times to cook evenly.

Transfer the pork to a cutting board. Discard any oil in the skillet and return the vegetables to the stove over high heat. Add the brandy and cook for 2 to 3 minutes, until the liquid almost evaporates entirely. Scrape the bottom of the pan with a spoon to loosen any stuck bits of meat and vegetables. Add the stock and cook for 3 to 5 minutes, until reduced by half. Strain the liquid into a small saucepan, add any juices from the pork that have collected on the plate, and whisk in the mustard. Cut the pork loin into thin slices, arrange on a plate, and spoon the mustard sauce over the pork.

Enjoy with Cakebread Cellars Merlot or a velvety merlot with coffee, red berry, cassis, and black pepper notes.

Venison Stew with Dried Cherries

We purchase venison from Broken Arrow Ranch in Central Texas. Mike Hughes, the owner of Broken Arrow, was one of the first purveyors at our American Harvest Workshop and has become a part of its history and our lives. He and his wife, Elizabeth, began their business nearly twenty years ago when they moved to the Texas Hill Country to raise their children. They farm deer, antelope, and other nontraditional livestock on their 700-acre ranch in Ingram, about sixty miles northwest of San Antonio. Venison has always been a meat we favor because of its relatively low fat content, and venison stew meat, like other red meat stew cuts, is ideal for slow cooking—the longer it simmers the more tender and succulent it becomes.

SERVES 4 TO 6

3 tablespoons extra virgin olive oil

2 pounds boneless venison stew meat, trimmed and cut into 1-inch cubes

Kosher salt

Freshly ground black pepper

1 large yellow onion, minced

1 stalk celery, minced

2 ounces prosciutto, minced

2 tablespoons tomato paste

1/4 cup all-purpose flour

2 cups cabernet sauvignon

2 cups brown chicken stock (page 210)

8 juniper berries, smashed

1 large bay leaf

1 (2-inch) length orange zest

3 large carrots (about 3/4 pound), peeled and cut into a large dice

1 1/2 pounds red potatoes, quartered

3/4 cup dried cherries

1/4 cup brandy

1 tablespoon chopped flat-leaf parsley, for garnish

Heat an enamel Dutch oven over high heat. Add 2 tablespoons of the olive oil. Season the venison with salt and pepper and add to the pot in batches so the pan is not overly full. Cook for about 10 minutes, or until browned on all sides, stirring once or twice. Transfer the venison to a plate with a slotted spoon.

Add the remaining 1 tablespoon olive oil, the onion, celery, and prosciutto to the pot. Cook for about 5 minutes, or until the onion begins to turn golden brown. Add the tomato paste and stir to mix. Sprinkle the flour over the top and stir until completely incorporated. Stir in the wine, scraping the bottom and sides of the pot. Add the stock, juniper berries, bay leaf, and orange zest. Bring to a boil. Add the venison and carrots and cover. Reduce the heat and cook on a low simmer for 1 1/2 hours, or until the meat is tender.

Add the potatoes, cherries, and brandy. Cook for 30 minutes, or until the potatoes are tender when pierced with a fork. Remove the bay leaf and orange zest. Season to taste with salt and pepper and sprinkle with the parsley.

Enjoy with Cakebread Cellars Benchland Select or Syrah, or an equally lush, elegant, fruit-forward red wine with soft tannins.

WINTER

Italian-Style Pot Roast

In southern Italy less-expensive cuts of meat have always dominated the kitchen because those regions have historically been less affluent than the north. To compensate for the tougher meat, dishes like this pot roast have been devised because the acid from the red wine and the tomatoes helps to tenderize the meat and add layers of flavor. Serve this with Traditional Soft Polenta (page 185) or Classic Mashed Potatoes (page 188).

SERVES 4 TO 6

2 tablespoons extra virgin olive oil

1 tablespoon unsalted butter

1 (3-pound) chuck roast

Kosher salt

Freshly ground black pepper

1 yellow onion, finely minced

1 carrot, peeled and finely minced

1 stalk celery, finely minced

2 cloves garlic, chopped

1 (28-ounce) can plum tomatoes, drained and chopped, liquid reserved

2 cups red wine

1/2 cup golden raisins

1/2 cup pine nuts

Preheat the oven to 350°.

Heat a Dutch oven over high heat. Add the olive oil and butter and cook until it stops foaming. Season the roast with salt and pepper and add to the pot. Cook for 3 to 4 minutes per side, until browned. Transfer the meat to a plate. Discard all but 2 tablespoons of the oil from the pot. Add the onion, carrot, and celery and cook for 4 to 5 minutes, until softened. Stir in the garlic. Add the tomatoes and the reserved juices and cook for 1 to 2 minutes. Add the wine and cook for 1 to 2 minutes. Add the meat, raisins, and pine nuts to the pot, cover, and bake for 2 hours, until the meat is tender, turning every 30 minutes or so to cook evenly.

Remove the meat from the oven and skim away and discard any of the fat that has risen to the top. Cook the liquid over high heat for 2 to 3 minutes, until thickened. Transfer the meat to a cutting board and cut into thin slices. Arrange on a warm serving platter and spoon the sauce over the top. Serve family style with polenta or mashed potatoes.

Enjoy with Cakebread Cellars Merlot, a hearty, robust wine, or another full-bodied red wine.

WINTER

Orange-Braised Chicken
with Bay Leaves and Black Olives

There are two types of bay leaves, the more common Turkish bay leaf, which is sold dried, and the California bay leaf, which can be found fresh and dried. Both smell and taste similar but we use only Turkish bay leaves in our dishes because we prefer their subtlety. To ensure that the dark meat pieces of the chicken get cooked but the breasts don't become dried out, the breasts are browned, removed from the pan, and then returned to finish cooking.

SERVES 4 TO 6

2 tablespoons extra virgin olive oil

1 small fryer chicken (about $3^1/2$ pounds), cut into 8 pieces

Kosher salt

Freshly ground black pepper

1 cup fresh orange juice

$^1/_4$ cup dry white wine

2 bay leaves

3 small dried red chiles

$^1/_2$ cup pitted oil-cured black olives, soaked in water for 1 hour

Heat the olive oil in a heavy-bottom stainless steel sauté pan or skillet over high heat. Season the chicken with salt and pepper and add to the pan. Cook for about 3 minutes per side, until browned. Transfer the breast pieces only to a plate. Push the remaining chicken pieces to one side of the pan and pour out any oil. Add the orange juice and wine to the pan and decrease the heat to low. Tuck the bay leaves and chiles between the chicken pieces. Cook, covered, on a low simmer for 10 minutes. Return the chicken breasts to the pan and cook for 10 minutes.

Transfer the chicken to a plate and increase the heat to high. Cook for 5 to 7 minutes, until the liquid becomes thick and syrupy. Return the chicken to the pot and toss to coat with the sauce. Add the olives and cook for 1 to 2 minutes. Serve hot.

Enjoy with Cakebread Cellars Rubaiyat, Napa Valley Chardonnay, or Pinot Noir. This is an incredibly wine-friendly dish that can be enjoyed with a variety of fine wines.

WINTER

Osso Buco

Osso Buco uses the same cooking method as a stew, yet it has a more elegant image. Ironically, its preparation is straightforward, but many people think of it as a special-occasion food and are always pleased when they find it on our dinner menu. We often serve it during the cold-weather months when we are entertaining. White wine is used to deglaze the pan, because veal is more delicate than beef and red wine can overpower the meat if it's added to the sauce. Serve with Traditional Soft Polenta (page 185).

SERVES 4

1/2 ounce dried porcini mushrooms

1 cup hot water

1/2 cup all-purpose flour

4 tablespoons extra virgin olive oil

1 tablespoon unsalted butter

4 large (about 3 inches thick) veal shanks

Kosher salt

Freshly ground black pepper

2 cloves garlic, chopped

4 large whole canned tomatoes, drained, squeezed, and chopped

1/2 cup dry white wine (such as sauvignon blanc)

1 cup chicken stock (page 212)

2 sprigs sage

4 large artichokes

1/2 lemon

1 tablespoon gremolata (page 212)

Preheat the oven to 350°.

Put the porcini mushrooms in a small bowl and cover with the hot water. Soak for 20 minutes, until rehydrated. Drain the porcini and chop, reserving the liquid. Strain the liquid through a fine-mesh sieve and set aside.

Put the flour in a shallow dish. Heat 2 tablespoons of the olive oil and the butter in a large, high-sided skillet or Dutch oven over high heat. Season the shanks with salt and pepper, add to the flour, and turn to lightly coat all sides. Add to the pan and cook for 2 to 3 minutes per side, until browned. Transfer to a plate and discard any remaining oil in the skillet. Return the skillet to high heat. Add the remaining 2 tablespoons olive oil and the garlic. Cook for 1 minute. Stir in the chopped porcini. Add the tomatoes and wine and cook for about 5 minutes. Return the meat to the skillet. Add the stock, reserved porcini liquid, and sage. Bring to a boil. Cover and bake for 2 hours, turning the meat every 30 minutes to cook evenly.

While the meat is cooking, prepare the artichokes. Fill a large bowl with water and squeeze the juice from the lemon into it. Add the lemon to the bowl. Cut off the stem and the leaves of the artichoke with a serrated knife, leaving only about 2 inches of the base. Trim away the green part of the stem with a paring knife. Cut around the sides, removing the dark green leaves until you reach the yellowish center. Scrape away the choke with a spoon. Cut each bottom in half and cut each half into 5 to 6 wedges. Place in the lemon water to keep the artichoke from turning brown. Repeat with all of the artichokes. Set aside.

When the meat has cooked for 2 hours, add the artichokes to the pot with the meat and cook for 30 minutes, until the artichokes are tender and the meat begins to fall away from the bones. Remove the shanks from the pan and bring the liquid to a boil over high heat. With the pan set slightly off the burner, skim away any foam or fat that rises to the top. Cook for 5 to 10 minutes, until the liquid begins to thicken. Return the meat to the skillet and cook until heated through. Stir in the gremolata. Serve over polenta.

Enjoy with Cakebread Cellars Cabernet Sauvignon or Merlot, or a full-bodied red wine with lots of berry, cherry, and plum flavors and with smooth tannins and hints of vanilla and spice.

WINTER

Vegetables &
Side Dishes

Grilled Asparagus with Fava Bean Pesto and Shaved Parmigiano-Reggiano

This is spring in a bite. When fava beans and asparagus begin to appear in the garden, this is one of the first dishes we serve. It's substantial enough that it can be served as a first course, but it also makes a wonderful side dish. Fava beans have an outer shell that is removed before cooking and a thin skin surrounding the beans that is peeled away before eating. It may seem like a lot of work, but it's worth it.

SERVES 4 TO 6

Kosher salt

$2^{1}/_{2}$ pounds fava beans, shelled

$1^{1}/_{4}$ to $1^{1}/_{2}$ cups extra virgin olive oil

$^{1}/_{2}$ cup grated Pecorino Romano

2 cloves garlic, chopped

1 teaspoon chopped fresh mint

Freshly ground black pepper

2 pounds asparagus, tough ends discarded

Parmigiano-Reggiano, for shaving

Light and heat a charcoal grill to medium heat.

Fill a medium saucepan with 8 cups of water. Add $^{1}/_{2}$ teaspoon of salt and bring to a boil over high heat. Add the fava beans and cook for about 1 minute, until tender to the bite. Transfer to a colander to drain. Rinse under cold water to stop any further cooking. Let cool.

Peel the skin off the fava beans and put the beans in the bowl of a food processor. Add $^{3}/_{4}$ cup of the olive oil, the Pecorino, garlic, and mint. Pulse to form a rough paste. If the mixture seems dry, add an additional $^{1}/_{4}$ cup olive oil in a slow, steady stream, until moist. Season to taste with salt and pepper. Set aside.

Set the asparagus on a baking sheet and brush with the remaining $^{1}/_{2}$ cup olive oil. Sprinkle with salt and pepper. Set on the grill and cook for about 5 minutes, until slightly charred on all sides. Turn frequently to cook evenly. Transfer to a warm plate and top with a spoonful of the fava bean pesto. Shave the Parmigiano over the top.

SPRING

Spinach with Raisins and Pine Nuts

In Southern Italy, and primarily in Sicily, raisins and pine nuts are often combined in savory dishes. The combination of sweet and nutty is especially delicious with spinach because of its slightly bitter taste. The entire dish becomes well-balanced, making it very wine friendly.

SERVES 4 TO 6

1 cup dry white wine (such as sauvignon blanc)

1 cup raisins

2 tablespoons extra virgin olive oil

2 cloves garlic, chopped

3 bunches (12 ounces each) spinach

$1/2$ cup toasted pine nuts

Kosher salt

Freshly ground black pepper

Fresh lemon juice

Combine the wine and raisins in a small saucepan. Bring to a boil over high heat. Remove from the heat and let sit for 20 minutes.

Heat the olive oil and garlic in a large nonstick skillet over high heat. Add the spinach and cook for 2 to 3 minutes, until wilted, stirring to cook evenly. Drain and add the raisins and pine nuts; stir to mix. Season to taste with salt, pepper, and lemon juice and serve.

SPRING

Celery Root Purée

People are often fooled by celery root purée. It looks like mashed potatoes, and that's what they expect. Instead, they get a bite of creamy, rich celery root, which, in this dish, tastes quite decadent because it is cooked in milk and then puréed until creamy smooth.

SERVES 4 TO 6

3 pounds celery root, peeled and cut into 1-inch cubes

4 cups whole milk

1 sprig thyme

$^1/_2$ teaspoon kosher salt

Put the celery root, milk, thyme, and salt in a large saucepan and bring to a boil over medium heat. Cook on a low simmer for 25 to 30 minutes, until the celery root is tender. Discard the thyme and transfer the celery root with a slotted spoon to a blender. Add $^1/_2$ cup of the milk. Put the lid on the blender and remove the vent cover on the top. Cover the vent with a towel to release steam. Purée until creamy, adding more milk as needed. Purée for about 5 minutes, until ultrasmooth, at first stopping occasionally to stir the mixture to evenly distribute the liquid.

Grilled Corn
with Chipotle and Lime

Jack loves to say that you can tell a real corn enthusiast by the way they cook it. He says that a real fan will put the water on the stove and then run out to the garden, pick the corn, clean it, and pop it in the pot when the water begins to boil, because the taste of fresh, just-picked corn can't be faked. That's true for this corn recipe. The fresher the corn the better.

SERVES 6

1/2 cup Chipotle-Lime Butter (page 212)

6 ears fresh corn

1 lime, cut into wedges

Kosher salt

Prepare the Chipotle-Lime Butter as directed.

Light and heat a charcoal grill to high heat. Pull the corn husks back to reveal the corn. Clean away any silk and then pull the husks back over the ear to cover the corn. Put the corn around the edge of the grill and cook for 6 to 8 minutes, until charred on all sides, turning frequently to cook evenly. Pull back the husks and spread a heaping tablespoon of the butter over each ear. Serve with the lime wedges and salt.

SUMMER

Zucchini and Mint–Stuffed Squash Blossoms

Both female and male blossoms grow on a zucchini plant. The fruit grows from the female blossom and the male is fruitless, which makes it ideal for cooking with. The blossoms should be picked early in the morning, when they are open, to make cleaning easier. Be careful when you pull out the pistil because the flowers are delicate and can tear easily.

SERVES 4 TO 6

8 to 12 squash blossoms

1 small zucchini, grated

$1/2$ teaspoon kosher salt

3 tablespoons extra virgin olive oil

1 small yellow onion, finely diced

2 ripe plum tomatoes, peeled, seeded, and finely diced

$1/4$ cup dried bread crumbs (page 215)

2 teaspoons chopped flat-leaf parsley

$1/2$ cup crumbled feta cheese

1 teaspoon finely shredded fresh mint leaves

Preheat the oven to 400°. Brush the bottom and sides of a large casserole dish with olive oil.

Trim the blossom stems to 1-inch lengths and carefully remove the pistils from the blossoms. Rinse the blossoms under cold water to remove any dirt that might be hiding in the folds of the petals. Set aside.

Set the zucchini in a large fine-mesh strainer set over a bowl or sink. Sprinkle with the salt and let sit for 20 minutes.

Heat 2 tablespoons of the olive oil and the onion in a small sauté pan over medium heat. Cook for about 6 minutes, until the onion is soft and translucent, stirring often to prevent browning. Add the tomatoes and cook for about 5 minutes, until the liquid is nearly evaporated, stirring often. Squeeze handfuls of the zucchini at a time to eliminate any excess moisture. Add to the onion mixture and cook for 2 to 3 minutes, until dry. Transfer to a bowl and let cool.

Combine the bread crumbs, the remaining 1 tablespoon olive oil, and the parsley in a small bowl. Set aside.

When the onion mixture is cool, stir the feta and mint into it. Scoop a heaping tablespoon of the onion mixture into a soup spoon and slide into the center of a blossom. Pinch together the ends. Arrange in the prepared baking dish and sprinkle 1 teaspoon of the bread crumb mixture over the top. Repeat with the remaining blossoms. Bake for 15 minutes, until the filling is warm and the bread crumbs are crunchy.

SUMMER

New Potatoes with
Extra Virgin Olive Oil and Fresh Herbs

Because of the forgiving climate of Napa Valley, we grow herbs year-round and cook with them every day. They add flavor to everything, including a simple potato. We especially like the contrast between the fresh herbs, the fruity olive oil, and the savory potatoes of this dish.

SERVES 4 TO 6

2 pounds small new potatoes

1 teaspoon kosher salt plus additional for seasoning

2 tablespoons extra virgin olive oil

1 tablespoon chopped fresh parsley

1 tablespoon chopped fresh chives

1 teaspoon chopped fresh thyme

Freshly ground black pepper

Cut a 1-inch strip of potato peel away from the center of the potato to create a decorative stripe in the center. Put the potatoes in a saucepan and cover with cold water. Add the 1 teaspoon salt and bring to a boil over high heat. Decrease the heat and cook on a simmer for 15 to 20 minutes, until tender when pierced with a knife. Drain and transfer to a small bowl. Add the olive oil, parsley, chives, and thyme. Stir to coat the potatoes evenly. Season to taste with salt and pepper and serve.

SUMMER

Haricot Vert with Roasted Shallots

Shallots, which are often overlooked by home cooks, are one of the most prized ingredients of chefs. They add flavor to a variety of foods, from vinaigrettes to sautés. When they are roasted for a long period of time, their sugars caramelize and the flavors intensify, which makes a great contrast to sturdy green beans.

SERVES 4 TO 6

12 ounces shallots, peeled and cut into $^1/_2$-inch pieces

$^1/_4$ cup extra virgin olive oil

2 tablespoons balsamic vinegar

Kosher salt

Freshly ground black pepper

8 ounces haricot vert, stem ends trimmed

Preheat the oven to 400°.

Put the shallots on a large piece of aluminum foil. Pour the olive oil and vinegar over the shallots. Sprinkle with a generous pinch of salt and pepper and toss to coat evenly. Fold and seal the foil to create a pouch. Set on a baking sheet and bake for 1 hour, until tender, browned, and caramelized.

While the shallots are cooking, heat a large pot of salted water to a boil over high heat. Add the haricot vert and cook for 2 to 3 minutes, until al dente. Transfer to a colander to drain, and rinse under cold water.

When the shallots are cooked, remove from the oven, open the foil, add the beans, and toss in the foil to mix well. Season to taste with salt and pepper and serve.

Caramelized Carrots with Cumin and River Ranch Honey

The carrots that we grow in our garden are the sweetest I've ever tasted. Carrots are fairly easy to cultivate and I strongly urge you to grow your own or seek out carrots from local farmers. There simply isn't a comparable substitute for freshly picked carrots. River Ranch honey is made from bees that pollinate our fruit orchard. Any good-quality honey is fine to use.

SERVES 4 TO 6

3 pounds garden-grown carrots, cut into 2-inch lengths on the diagonal

2 tablespoons extra virgin olive oil

1 teaspoon ground cumin

1 teaspoon kosher salt

2 cloves garlic, cut into slivers

1 tablespoon River Ranch honey (or any quality honey)

Combine the carrots, olive oil, cumin, and salt in large skillet over medium heat. Cover to allow the carrots to release their juices and produce steam. Cook for 15 to 20 minutes, shaking the pan occasionally to stir the ingredients, until the carrots are tender. Remove the cover, increase the heat to high, and cook for about 10 minutes, until the liquid evaporates and the carrots develop a shiny glaze. Add the garlic and cook for 2 to 3 minutes, stirring frequently, until the carrots are browned. Add the honey and toss to coat evenly. Cook for 3 to 4 minutes, stirring constantly. Serve immediately.

FALL

Couscous with Currants and Toasted Almonds

Couscous is a Middle Eastern comfort food. The traditional cooking method requires multiple cooking steps using a special steamer. This quick version cooks faster than almost any other type of pasta, can be enhanced with everything from fruits to vegetables, and is a great choice as a bed for seafood, meat, and poultry. The trick to making couscous is to make it in a wide pot, as it has a tendency to clump.

SERVES 4

$^1/_2$ cup currants

2 cups water

2 tablespoons extra virgin olive oil

1 teaspoon kosher salt plus additional for seasoning

2 cups couscous

1 cup sliced almonds, toasted

Freshly ground black pepper

Put the currants in a small bowl. Cover with hot water and let sit for 15 minutes. Drain.

Combine the water, olive oil, and salt in a small saucepan. Bring to a boil over high heat. Add the couscous, cover, remove from the heat, and let steam for 15 minutes. Fluff the couscous with a fork. Add the currants and almonds. Season to taste with salt and pepper.

Wilted Cabbage Slaw
with Chorizo

Chorizo, the Spanish word for all types of sausage, is usually sold as a fresh, spicy pork sausage in the United States. The quality and ingredients vary from producer to producer. The best choice is to buy from a well-known sausage maker in your area that uses high-quality, freshly ground pork.

SERVES 4 TO 6

$^1/_2$ cup toasted pumpkin seeds (page 214)

$^1/_2$ large head (about 1 pound) green cabbage, grated

1 carrot, peeled and grated

1 teaspoon kosher salt plus additional for seasoning

$^3/_4$ pound (3 links) chorizo sausage, casings discarded

1 tablespoon extra virgin olive oil

2 tablespoons sherry vinegar

$^1/_2$ cup chopped cilantro

Freshly ground black pepper

Prepare the pumpkin seeds as directed.

Put the cabbage and carrot in a large colander set over a bowl or sink and sprinkle with the 1 teaspoon salt. Let sit for 20 minutes.

Heat a skillet over high heat. Add the chorizo and olive oil, breaking the sausage into pieces with the back of a wooden spoon. Cook for 4 to 5 minutes, until browned. Set aside.

Rinse the cabbage mixture and squeeze it between your hands to remove any excess liquid; transfer to a large bowl. Add the sausage to the cabbage and then add the vinegar and cilantro and stir to mix well. Stir in the pumpkin seeds. Season to taste with salt and pepper.

FALL

Roasted Root Vegetables
with Balsamic Vinegar

Root vegetables are the most humble crops of the garden, probably due to their mundane appearance. Roasting brings forth their goodness. They become sweeter, crisp on the outside, and tender on the inside. This recipe further enhances the sweetness of the vegetables with the addition of balsamic vinegar. Sparrow Lane Vinegars produces outstanding vinegar that we always keep stocked in our pantry. For many years, owners Phil and Denise Toohey have participated in our American Harvest Workshop, introducing chefs to their fine vinegars, including their traditional balsamic and their innovative golden balsamic vinegar.

SERVES 4 TO 6

2 large parsnips, peeled, quartered, cored, and cut
    into 1-inch lengths

2 turnips, peeled and cut into 1-inch chunks

1 rutabaga, peeled and cut into 1-inch chunks

2 large carrots, peeled, halved, and cut into 1-inch lengths

12 ounces small beets, peeled and quartered

1/4 cup extra virgin olive oil

1/4 cup balsamic vinegar

Kosher or sea salt

Freshly ground black pepper

Preheat the oven to 400°.

Put the parsnips, turnips, rutabaga, carrots, and beets in a roasting pan large enough to hold the vegetables in a single layer. Pour the olive oil over the vegetables and toss to coat evenly. Bake for 45 minutes, or until the vegetables are almost tender and the juices are caramelized. Pour the balsamic vinegar over the vegetables and sprinkle with a generous amount of salt and pepper. Toss to coat evenly. Return to the oven and bake for 10 to 15 minutes, stirring once or twice to distribute the juices evenly during cooking. Season to taste with salt and pepper.

Oven-Roasted Yukon Potatoes

Don't be afraid of the generous portion of olive oil used in this recipe. It is what makes the potatoes crispy and adds flavor. Yukon gold potatoes are the best choice, but you can also use other yellow-fleshed potatoes, such as fingerlings or new potatoes. Be sure that the oven is completely preheated before putting the potatoes in or they won't get as crispy.

SERVES 4 TO 6

3 pounds small Yukon gold potatoes, quartered

^{1}/4 cup extra virgin olive oil

1 teaspoon fresh thyme leaves

1 teaspoon kosher salt

Freshly ground black pepper

Preheat the oven to 425°.

Toss the potatoes and olive oil together in a bowl. Spread on a baking sheet in a single layer. Bake for 30 minutes. Remove from the oven and sprinkle with the thyme, salt, and pepper. Stir and return to the oven. Bake for 15 minutes, until the potatoes are crispy and browned. Serve warm.

WINTER

Traditional Soft Polenta

In the last few decades, American cooks have elevated polenta to a noble food. Considered peasant food for centuries in Italy, polenta is now praised globally for its versatility and taste. It can be served soft or firm and is a great side dish for all kinds of meats and stews.

SERVES 4 TO 6

6 cups water

1 teaspoon kosher salt

1 1/2 cups coarsely ground cornmeal

1/2 cup freshly grated Parmigiano-Reggiano

Kosher salt

Freshly ground black pepper

Bring the water and salt to a boil in a large saucepan over high heat. Whisk in the cornmeal in a steady stream. Decrease the heat to low and continue whisking occasionally for the first 5 minutes. Cook for 20 to 25 minutes, until the polenta is tender and creamy, stirring occasionally with a wooden spoon. Stir in the Parmigiano and season to taste with salt and pepper.

For grilled polenta: After the polenta is cooked and the cheese has been added, spread out on an oiled baking sheet and refrigerate until firm. Cut the polenta into 3-inch triangles. Place the triangles on a gas or charcoal grill heated to high and cook for 3 minutes, until grill marks appear. Turn and grill the other side for 2 minutes until grill marks appear and the center is warm.

WINTER

American Harvest Workshop Recipe

David Koelling's Winter Squash Purée

David Koelling, a chef filled with wanderlust, had cooked all over the country by the time he joined us at the workshop in 1990. His intrinsic talent for turning local ingredients into unforgettable dishes made him a pioneer in regional American cuisine. He prepared this squash purée with wild boar bacon from Broken Arrow Ranch when he cooked it at the workshop, but a good smoked bacon with a balance of sweet, tangy, and smoky flavors will be a fine substitute.

SERVES 4 TO 6

3 pounds winter squash (such as hubbard, butternut, or kabocha), peeled, seeded, and cut into 1-inch chunks (8 cups)

1 cup water

6 ounces wild boar bacon or applewood-smoked bacon

1 yellow onion, finely chopped

$1/2$ cup dark brown sugar

$1/2$ cup apple cider vinegar

1 to 2 tablespoons unsalted butter

Kosher salt

Freshly ground black pepper

Put the squash in a high-sided skillet and add the water. Heat over medium-low heat, covered, and cook for 20 to 25 minutes, until the squash is tender.

While the squash is cooking, mince the bacon in a food processor. Combine with the onion in a nonstick sauté pan over high heat and cook for 8 to 10 minutes, until the onion is translucent. Add the brown sugar and stir to dissolve. Cook for about 5 minutes, until the liquid evaporates and the mixture becomes thick and dark brown. Add the vinegar and cook for 3 to 4 minutes, until reduced by half. Set aside.

Transfer the squash and the bacon mixture to a food processor in batches and purée. Add the butter. Pulse to combine. Season to taste with salt and pepper. Serve warm.

WINTER

Classic Mashed Potatoes

Everyone loves mashed potatoes, although it is possible no one loves them as much as Jack does. They are by far one of his favorite dishes. These have a silky texture because they are put through a food mill. If you don't have a food mill you can use a ricer or an old-fashioned hand-held masher; they will just be a little less creamy.

SERVES 4 TO 6

4 russet potatoes (3^1/$_2$ to 4 pounds), unpeeled

1 teaspoon kosher salt plus additional for seasoning

6 tablespoons unsalted butter

1 to 1^1/$_2$ cups milk

Freshly ground black pepper

Put the potatoes in a large saucepan. Cover with cold water and add the 1 teaspoon salt. Bring to a boil over high heat. Decrease the heat and cook on a simmer for 25 minutes, until tender when pierced with a knife. Drain. While still hot, hold the potatoes in a clean towel and peel with a paring knife. Press through a food mill into a saucepan. Add the butter and stir to combine. Stir in 1 cup of the milk, adding more as needed to produce a soft consistency. Season with salt and pepper. Serve immediately or place a piece of plastic wrap directly on the potatoes and set the pan in a warm water bath for up to 1 hour before serving.

WINTER

Red Wine—Braised Cabbage

Savory, with just the right amount of zing, this cabbage dish is perfect for serving with braised or roasted meat, especially pork. And, like most dishes that are cooked with wine, it is especially wine friendly. It can be prepared a day ahead, refrigerated, and reheated when ready to serve.

SERVES 4 TO 6

2 tablespoons extra virgin olive oil

2 yellow onions, halved and cut into thin slices lengthwise

1 head red cabbage (about 2$\frac{1}{2}$ pounds), shredded

1 teaspoon kosher salt

$\frac{1}{4}$ teaspoon ground cloves

2 tart apples (such as Granny Smith or pippin), peeled, cored, and grated

2 cups light, fruity dry red wine (such as Rubaiyat or pinot noir)

1 tablespoon red wine vinegar

Heat the olive oil in a wide-bottom stockpot over medium heat. Add the onions and cook for 1 minute. Add the cabbage, salt, and cloves and stir to mix well. Cook for 30 minutes, until the cabbage and onions are completely wilted. Add the apples, wine, and vinegar. Cover and cook for 45 minutes, until the cabbage is soft. Remove the lid, increase the heat to high, and cook for 2 to 3 minutes, stirring, until the cabbage is evenly coated with the liquid. Serve warm.

WINTER

Desserts

Seasonal Cheese Course

We serve a cheese course with almost every meal and in every season at the winery. Because we serve a progression of wines with a meal, we like to showcase the last wine, which is usually one of our vineyard-designate or older wines. This relaxed setting allows everyone to savor every nuance of the wine and to fully enjoy the cheese.

Our cheese course is always served family style on a large board because it encourages interaction and sharing among our guests. The cheese platter is garnished with thin slices of toasted baguettes (follow the recipe for crostini on page 44). Seasonal garnishes are also served, including toasted nuts, sliced pears, grapes, and fresh berries.

A typical cheese course usually includes three cheeses of varying styles, such as a hard cheese, a soft, bloomy rind cheese, and a blue-veined cheese. We serve approximately one ounce of each type of cheese for each person. This is a general rule of thumb, and can be increased or decreased. We serve only American cheeses and usually those produced by local, artisanal cheese makers. Here are some of our favorites:

Hard cheese: Vella's dry jack, Winchester Gouda, or Mato's St. George.
Soft, bloomy rind cheese: Redwood Hill's Camelia or Cowgirl Creamery's Mount Tam or Pierce Point.
Blue-veined cheese: Point Reyes Blue or Hubbardston Blue Logs.

Honey Ice Cream
with Candied Walnuts

The candied walnuts that are added to this ice cream were inspired by a recipe from Hugh Carpenter, a cookbook author and cooking teacher in the Napa Valley who often hosts cooking classes at the winery. The ice cream is incredibly airy, sweet, and delectable.

SERVES 4 TO 6

3 cups milk

1 cup honey

3 cups heavy whipping cream

1 cup candied walnuts, coarsely chopped (page 211)

Prepare an ice-cream maker according to the manufacturer's directions.

Combine the milk and honey in a small saucepan. Heat over medium heat for 5 minutes, until the honey is dissolved, stirring constantly. Pour into a bowl and refrigerate for at least 2 hours, or until chilled.

Whip the cream in a medium bowl until soft peaks form. Fold into the milk mixture and pour into the ice-cream maker. Freeze according to manufacturer's directions, being careful not to overchurn or it will become icy. It's best to churn as close to serving as possible to avoid crystallization. When firm, transfer to a bowl and stir in the nuts. Scoop into bowls and serve.

Polenta Cheesecake with Strawberries Macerated in Zinfandel

This is a rare dessert in that it can be paired with wine. Because the strawberries are macerated in the wine and served as a sauce with the cake, they balance out the sweetness of the cake and make it wine friendly. This recipe was developed when we made our Howell Mountain Zinfandel, which we hope to produce again soon.

SERVES 4 TO 6

2 cups ricotta cheese

2 cups mascarpone

1¼ cups granulated sugar

1 tablespoon anise seed, crushed

1 teaspoon pure vanilla extract

¾ cup polenta (coarse ground cornmeal)

2 pints strawberries, hulled and thinly sliced

½ cup dry red wine (such as zinfandel or pinot noir)

Confectioners' sugar, for dusting

Preheat the oven to 300°. Butter a 10-inch springform pan.

Whisk together the ricotta, mascarpone, 1 cup of the sugar, the anise seed, and vanilla in a large mixing bowl. Add the polenta and mix well. Pour into the prepared springform pan and spread out with a spatula. Bake for 1 to 1¼ hours. The center should still tremble slightly.

While the cake is baking, put the strawberries in a large bowl and toss with the remaining ¼ cup sugar. Add the red wine and stir to mix. Let sit at room temperature for 30 to 40 minutes. (Refrigerate after 40 minutes or the strawberries will begin to break down.)

Preheat the broiler. Remove the side of the springform pan. Place the cake under the broiler for 2 to 3 minutes, until lightly browned. Dust with the confectioners' sugar and cut into slices. Spread a small spoonful of the strawberries in the center of each serving dish and top with a slice of cake.

Enjoy with Cakebread Cellars Rubaiyat or Pinot Noir, or a light red wine with bright fruit flavors.

🌿 SPRING

Strawberry and Rhubarb Galette

Rhubarb is a symbol of spring. Although for years it was much loved in the northeastern part of the United States, rhubarb didn't reach culinary popularity in the rest of the country until Luther Burbank, a Sonoma County botanist, developed a variety with a longer season and a milder taste. As raw rhubarb can be quite sour and unpleasant, it is almost always cooked and is usually used in desserts that are sweetened with sugar. It is often combined with strawberries, as it is in this recipe, because they lend added sweetness for balance.

SERVES 6

DOUGH

1 cup all-purpose flour

1 teaspoon sugar

Kosher salt

6 tablespoons cold, unsalted butter, cut into small pieces

1/4 cup ice water

FILLING

1/4 cup plus 1 tablespoon sliced almonds

3 tablespoons sugar

1 tablespoon all-purpose flour

1 pint strawberries, hulled and sliced

2 large stalks rhubarb, cut into 1/2-inch-thick slices

1 egg, beaten

To make the dough: Combine the flour, sugar, and a pinch of salt in the bowl of an electric mixer fitted with the paddle attachment. Add the butter and mix until the dough is the size of peas. Add the ice water and mix until the dough sticks together. Transfer to a large piece of plastic wrap. Shape into a round disk, wrap tightly, and refrigerate for 1 hour.

Preheat the oven to 375°.

Roll out the dough on a floured surface to a large circle 1/8 inch thick. Trim the edges to make a smooth circle. Transfer to a parchment paper–lined baking sheet.

To make the filling: Add the 1/4 cup almonds, 2 tablespoons of the sugar, and the flour to the bowl of a food processor and process until a fine mixture is achieved. Spread out in the center of the dough, leaving a 2-inch border. Combine the strawberries, rhubarb, and remaining 1 tablespoon sugar in a medium bowl. Spread over the almond mixture. Fold the edge of the dough over the filling, folding it into creases as you work around the entire circle.

Bake for 25 to 30 minutes, until golden brown. Remove from the oven and brush the dough with the egg. Sprinkle the 1 tablespoon almonds over the dough and return to the oven to bake for 15 minutes. Let cool before slicing. Serve with ice cream or freshly whipped cream.

🌺 SPRING

Individual Amaretti Cookie Soufflés
with Strawberry Sauce

We love to enjoy these soufflés after a meal with a cup of coffee. The amaretti cookies give the soufflés a nice almond flavor and crunchy texture. The strawberry sauce can be made ahead of time and refrigerated for up to three days or frozen for up to one month. If you have leftover sauce you can pour it over ice cream or a bowl of mixed berries.

SERVES 6

1/2 cup granulated sugar plus additional for coating

1 1/2 cups milk

1/3 cup all-purpose flour

3 egg yolks

1 tablespoon dark rum

2 cups strawberries, hulled and halved

Fresh lemon juice

4 egg whites

3/4 cup crushed amaretti cookies

Confectioners' sugar

Preheat the oven to 400°. Butter the sides and bottoms of six 6-ounce ramekins. Coat lightly with granulated sugar. Put on a baking sheet and set aside.

Heat 1 cup of the milk in a small saucepan over medium heat. Whisk together the remaining 1/2 cup milk and the flour in a small bowl. Whisk into the warm milk and bring to a boil, whisking continuously. Transfer to a small bowl and whisk in 1/4 cup of the sugar, the egg yolks, and rum. (The recipe can be prepared up to 4 hours in advance up to this point. Set a piece of plastic wrap directly on the top of the mixture and refrigerate. Bring to room temperature before completing.)

Combine the strawberries and 2 tablespoons of the sugar in a small saucepan. Cover and cook over medium heat for 3 to 5 minutes, until the berries become soft. Transfer to a blender and purée. Adjust the sweetness to taste with lemon juice.

Whip the egg whites in a medium bowl until soft peaks form. Add the remaining 2 tablespoons sugar and beat until stiff peaks form. Fold one-third of the egg whites into the egg yolk mixture to make it lighter. Fold back into the egg whites. Fold in the cookies and fill each ramekin three-quarters full. Bake for 25 minutes, until the soufflés have risen above the lips of the ramekins and are lightly browned. Dust with the confectioners' sugar and transfer to plates. Insert a spoon into the center of each one. Pour a small amount of the strawberry sauce into the center and serve immediately.

SPRING

Charentais Melon with Rubaiyat and Raspberries

Charentais melons are sometimes called a French cantelope. They are an heirloom melon, with orange flesh, light skin, and a musky aroma, and are one of the sweetest and most aromatic types of melon. They grow in hot, dry areas, which is why they do so well in our garden and in their place of origin, the south of France. There, a dish similar to this one is made with Banyuls, a wine produced in the same area. Melons do not ripen further once they are picked, but they do show signs of age quickly, so buy the sweetest-smelling melon you can find and eat it as soon as possible.

SERVES 4 TO 6

1¹/₂ cups Cakebread Cellars Rubaiyat or other fruity, light red wine

1 heaping cup fresh raspberries plus additional for garnish

¹/₂ cup sugar

1 (2-inch length) vanilla bean

2 to 3 charentais melons (about 2 pounds each), unpeeled, halved, seeded, and chilled

Combine the wine, the 1 cup raspberries, the sugar, and vanilla bean in a small saucepan. Bring to a boil over medium heat. Cook on a low simmer for 5 to 10 minutes, until reduced by one-quarter. Strain through a fine-mesh strainer, pushing down on the berries to extract all of the liquid, and refrigerate until cool.

Arrange the melon halves in shallow bowls and pour a small amount of the wine mixture into the center of each melon. Add a few raspberries and serve.

Enjoy with Cakebread Cellars Rubaiyat or a light, fruity, red wine.

Plum and Red Wine Sorbetto

The time to make this sorbet is when plums are at the peak of their season and so sweet and ripe that the skin melts in your mouth. Its gorgeous fuchsia color is so intense that it readies your palate for the rich flavor impact the dessert makes, bite after bite. We like the robust flavor of Santa Rosa plums in this recipe.

SERVES 6

1 cup red wine

1/2 cup water

1/2 cup sugar

4 large red plums, pitted and cut into pieces

1 to 2 tablespoons fresh lemon juice

Kosher salt

Prepare an ice-cream maker according to the manufacturer's directions.

Combine the wine, water, sugar, and plums in a large saucepan. Bring to a boil over high heat. Cook for 5 minutes, until the plums soften. Remove from the heat. Transfer to a blender. Remove the vent cover from the top and cover the vent with a towel to let the steam escape. Purée. Add 1 tablespoon of the lemon juice and a pinch of salt while blending. Pour into a wide, shallow bowl and refrigerate for 1 to 2 hours, or until thoroughly chilled. Taste again and add more lemon juice if too sweet.

Freeze according to manufacturer's directions. Scoop into bowls and serve.

🌿 SUMMER

American Harvest Workshop Recipe

Mark Franz's Roasted Peaches with Fromage Blanc

Mark Franz is one of San Francisco's most respected chefs. In 2002, when he joined us for our workshop, we were bowled over by his professional integrity, his spirit, and his passion for his craft. Mark cooked at some of the best restaurants in the Bay Area, including the renowned Stars, before opening Farallon, a restaurant where he renders humble seafood into classic dishes with the touch of an alchemist. One of the great joys of the workshop is watching chefs apply their talents to something so modest as a peach and convert it into greatness with only a few ingredients, as Mark did with this extraordinary dessert.

SERVES 6

$1/2$ cup almonds

$1/2$ cup extra virgin olive oil

3 large ripe peaches

1 teaspoon fresh thyme leaves

Coarsely ground black pepper

$3/4$ cup fromage blanc or fresh ricotta cheese

6 tablespoons heavy whipping cream

1 tablespoon honey

Preheat the oven to 450°.

Put the almonds in a small saucepan and cover with water. Bring to a boil over high heat. Cook for 2 minutes. Drain and let cool. Peel the almonds.

Heat the olive oil in a small saucepan over medium heat, until the surface shimmers. Add the almonds and increase the heat to medium-high. Cook for 10 to 15 minutes, until the almonds are evenly browned, stirring constantly. Let cool.

Cut the peaches in half, remove the stones, and place the peaches in a large bowl. Add 2 tablespoons of olive oil from the almonds, the thyme, and a pinch of black pepper. Toss gently to coat well. Arrange on a baking dish, cut side up, and bake for 10 to 15 minutes, until lightly browned and tender but not too soft.

Combine the fromage blanc, cream, and honey in a bowl. Stir until smooth. Divide the cheese mixture among the serving dishes. Place a peach half in the center of each bowl over the cheese. Chop the almonds and sprinkle in the center of the peach. Sprinkle a few grains of pepper over the peaches and serve.

SUMMER

Hazelnut and Chocolate Semifreddo

Sharffen Berger Chocolate Maker was founded by a former doctor, Robert Steinberg, and a winemaker, John Scharffenberger. After Robert became intrigued by the idea of making his own chocolate and set off to learn about every aspect of such an enterprise, the two began to produce extraordinary, high-quality chocolate for eating and cooking. One of the unique items they produce is cacao nibs, which are roasted cocoa beans separated from their husks and broken into small bits. They aren't as sweet as chocolate chips, but they are a delicious addition to sweet dishes like this one. This recipe needs about four hours in the freezer to set, so if you plan on serving it the same day you make it, plan ahead.

SERVES 4 TO 6

SEMIFREDDO

3 ounces toasted hazelnuts, chopped

$1/2$ cup plus 2 tablespoons sugar

6 egg yolks, at room temperature

$1/4$ cup Marsala

1 cup heavy whipping cream

4 egg whites, at room temperature

$1/2$ cup cacao nibs or chopped bittersweet chocolate

CHOCOLATE SAUCE

1 cup water

$1/2$ cup sugar

$1/2$ cup cocoa powder

2 ounces bittersweet chocolate, chopped

To make the semifreddo: Line the bottom and sides of a 9-inch loaf pan with waxed paper, leaving a few inches of paper hanging over the sides.

Grind the hazelnuts and $1/4$ cup of the sugar together in the bowl of a food processor. Set aside.

Fill a large saucepan 1 inch deep with water. Bring to a boil over medium heat. Put the egg yolks, $1/4$ cup of the sugar, and the Marsala in a large stainless steel bowl that will rest on top of the pan without touching the water. Set the bowl over the pan and beat with a whisk for about 5 minutes, until thick and frothy. (It should be able to hold a ribbon when the whisk is moved back and forth across the surface.) Remove from the heat and set in an ice water bath until chilled.

Whip the cream in a large bowl with a whisk until soft peaks form. Fold in the hazelnut mixture and cacao nibs and then fold this into the egg yolk mixture.

In a medium bowl, whip the egg whites with the 2 tablespoons sugar until stiff peaks form and the egg whites are glossy. Fold into the whipped cream and egg yolk mixture. Pour into the prepared loaf pan and fold the extra paper over the top of the mixture. Freeze for 4 hours, or until firm.

To make the chocolate sauce: Combine the water and sugar in a saucepan. Bring to a boil over high heat and cook for about 5 minutes, until the sugar dissolves. Stir in the cocoa powder. Remove from the heat and add the chocolate. Stir until smooth. Refrigerate until ready to use.

Remove the semifreddo from the loaf pan, cut into slices, and arrange on serving dishes. Pour a small amount of the chocolate sauce over the top and sides in a decorative pattern. Serve immediately.

🌸 FALL

Poached Pears with Caramel Sauce

The pears for this silky, seductive dessert can be made a day ahead and refrigerated in their cooking liquid. The caramel sauce, too, can be made three to four days ahead, and stored in an airtight container. Just reheat in a bowl set over a pot of hot water. Be careful making the caramel sauce; once it begins to brown it can burn quickly and it is very hot, so take care not to spill it.

SERVES 6

PEARS

2 cups water

1 cup dry white wine

1/2 cup honey

1/4 cup sugar

3 (1/4-inch) slices peeled ginger

1 (2-inch length) vanilla bean

1 cinnamon stick

3 ripe pears (about 1/2 pound each), peeled

CARAMEL SAUCE

1 cup sugar

1/2 cup water

1/2 cup heavy whipping cream

To make the pears: Combine the water, wine, honey, sugar, ginger, vanilla bean, and cinnamon in a saucepan small enough to submerge the pears in the liquid. Stir until the sugar dissolves. Add the pears and bring to a simmer over medium heat. Decrease the heat to low and cook on a low simmer for 20 to 30 minutes, or until the pears are tender. Let cool in the liquid.

To make the sauce: Combine the sugar and water in a small saucepan over high heat. Bring to a boil and cook for 8 to 10 minutes, until dark brown, gently swirling the pan occasionally to evenly distribute the heat. Remove from the heat, add the cream carefully (it will bubble up), and stir vigorously until the mixture stops bubbling. Transfer to a bowl, cover with plastic wrap, and refrigerate.

Cut the pears in half, remove the core, and cut each half into thin slices, keeping the top intact. Fan out each pear half on a plate and drizzle with the caramel sauce.

FALL

Apple Cranberry Crisp

The quintessential autumn dessert, this old-fashioned crisp is very rustic and comforting. Plus, you get all the benefits of apple pie without the added effort of making crusts. Serve it with a dollop of crème fraîche or vanilla ice cream.

SERVES 4 TO 6

4 large Granny Smith apples, peeled, cored, and cut into $1^1/_2$-inch cubes

1 (12-ounce) package fresh cranberries

$^2/_3$ cup plus $^3/_4$ cup sugar

$^1/_2$ cup (1 stick) plus 2 tablespoons unsalted butter, cut into pieces

1 cup all-purpose flour

1 cup rolled oats

$^1/_2$ teaspoon ground cinnamon

Preheat the oven to 375°.

Combine the apples and cranberries in a 14-inch, shallow, oval baking dish. Sprinkle the $^2/_3$ cup sugar over the fruit and toss with your hands to evenly coat the fruit. Put the $^3/_4$ cup sugar, the butter, and flour into the bowl of a food processor. Pulse until the mixture becomes the size of small peas. Add the oats and cinnamon and pulse to combine. Spread over the top of the fruit. Bake for 45 minutes to 1 hour, until the topping is browned and crispy. Serve warm.

FALL

Cornmeal and Ginger Shortbread Cookies

The cornmeal added to this cookie dough gives these cookies extra crunch. They are very sweet and make a lovely dessert by themselves or served with ice cream or sorbet. The cookies will remain pale when cooked and might feel slightly soft when they are first removed from the oven, but they will crisp up as they cool.

MAKES APPROXIMATELY 36 COOKIES

1 cup (2 sticks) unsalted butter, at room temperature

$2/3$ cup confectioners' sugar

1 tablespoon peeled and grated fresh ginger

1 teaspoon pure vanilla extract

$1^1/2$ cups all-purpose flour

$1/2$ cup fine cornmeal

$1/4$ teaspoon salt

Preheat the oven to 350°. Line a baking sheet with parchment paper.

Beat the butter with the back of a wooden spoon in a large mixing bowl until smooth. Add the sugar, ginger, and vanilla and stir until smooth. Add the flour, cornmeal, and salt and stir until the dry ingredients are completely incorporated. Shape into a flat disk and refrigerate for 20 minutes.

Put the dough on a lightly floured work surface and roll out to $1/4$ inch thick. Cut into 2-inch squares or circles using a cookie cutter. Arrange on the prepared baking sheet and bake for 20 to 25 minutes, until golden brown. Let cool on a rack.

Cabernet Truffles

There are times after a gratifying meal when all that is needed is one bite of something sweet. These luscious truffles are perfect for such an occasion. We sometimes serve them after dessert if it is a special event, or offer them to guests as a treat to take home. These are one of the few desserts we serve with a dry red wine, because wine is used to flavor them. They taste especially delicious with our reserve cabernet wines because the tannins have softened, leaving lots of fruit flavors that really sparkle in conjunction with the rich chocolate.

SERVES 4 TO 6

8 ounces bittersweet chocolate, broken into pieces

6 tablespoons unsalted butter, cut into pieces, at room temperature

2 tablespoons heavy whipping cream

1/4 cup cabernet sauvignon

1/2 cup unsweetened cocoa powder

Melt the chocolate in the top of a double boiler set over a pan of hot water. Remove from the heat. Add the butter and cream and stir until smooth. Stir in the wine. Transfer to an 8-inch nonstick loaf pan, cover tightly with plastic wrap, and refrigerate for 1 1/2 hours, or until firm.

Put the cocoa powder in a small bowl or pie tin.

Remove the chocolate mixture from the refrigerator and shape into small balls (about 1 inch in diameter) using the small end of a melon baller. (To make the shaping easier, dip the melon baller in hot water before and between shaping.) Arrange the balls on a plate and refrigerate for 2 to 3 minutes, or until firm and dry. Drop the truffles into the cocoa and roll them around to coat completely. Repeat until all of the chocolate is used.

The truffles can be stored in an airtight container in the refrigerator for up to one week. Let stored truffles sit at room temperature for 20 minutes before serving.

Enjoy with Cakebread Cellars Cabernet Sauvignon Reserve or another cabernet sauvignon with soft tannins and lots of cherry and berry flavors.

WINTER

Profiteroles with Bittersweet Chocolate Sorbet and Raspberry Sauce

The sorbet in this dessert is so intense that it belies its simple composition of water, sugar, and chocolate. We use only Scharffen Berger chocolate because it has a richness that is uncommon and truly affects the taste of the dish it is added to. Scharffen Berger makes a variety of chocolate products, including both the cocoa powder and the bittersweet chocolate that we use in this sorbet.

MAKES APPROXIMATELY 18 PROFITEROLES

RASPBERRY SAUCE

12 ounces fresh or frozen raspberries

2 cups dry red wine

$1/2$ cup sugar

SORBET

2 cups water

$1/2$ cup sugar

$1/2$ cup cocoa powder

2 ounces bittersweet chocolate, chopped

PROFITEROLES

1 cup water

$1/2$ cup (1 stick) unsalted butter, diced

1 cup all-purpose flour

4 large eggs

Kosher salt

Confectioners' sugar, for dusting

Prepare an ice-cream maker according to the manufacturer's directions.

To make the raspberry sauce: Combine the raspberries, wine, and sugar in a nonreactive saucepan and bring to a boil over high heat. Reduce the heat to medium-high and cook for 20 to 30 minutes, until the liquid is reduced by half. Strain through a fine-mesh sieve set over a bowl, pressing down to release all of the liquid from the berries. Refrigerate until chilled.

To make the sorbet: Combine the water and sugar in a small saucepan and bring to a boil over high heat. Cook for 1 minute, until the sugar dissolves. Remove from the heat and whisk in the cocoa powder. Whisk for 1 to 2 minutes, until completely blended. Let cool for 5 minutes. Put the chocolate in a bowl. Pour the sugar mixture over the chocolate and stir until smooth. Refrigerate for at least 30 minutes, or set in an ice water bath until thoroughly chilled.

Pour the chocolate mixture into the ice-cream maker and freeze according to the manufacturer's directions.

While the sorbet is freezing, make the profiteroles. Preheat the oven to 400°. Line a baking sheet with parchment paper.

Bring the water and butter to a boil in a large, heavy-bottom saucepan over medium-high heat. Remove from the heat. Add the flour all at once and stir until the ingredients form a mass. Return to the heat and continue cooking and stirring for 1 to 2 minutes. Remove from the heat and transfer to the bowl of an electric mixer fitted with the paddle attachment. Run for 2 to 3 minutes to release steam and let cool. With the mixer running on high speed, add the eggs, one at a time, until each is fully incorporated and the dough is smooth. Add a small pinch of salt.

Transfer the dough to a pastry bag fitted with a $1/2$-inch tip. Pipe mounds 1 to $1^1/_2$ inches in diameter 1 inch apart on the prepared baking sheet. Smooth down the tip left from the pastry bag with a wet finger. Bake for 30 to 35 minutes, until golden brown. Turn off the oven and let the pastries sit in the oven for about 1 hour, until completely dry.

Cut the pastry puffs in half horizontally and scoop a small amount of the sorbet into the center of each. Replace the top half over the sorbet. Spoon a small amount of the raspberry sauce into the center of each plate. Set three profiteroles over the sauce and sprinkle with confectioners' sugar. Serve immediately.

Appendices

Basic Recipes & Techniques

RECIPES

Aioli

YIELD: ABOUT 1 CUP

1 clove garlic, peeled and coarsely chopped

$^1/_4$ teaspoon kosher salt

1 egg yolk

1 tablespoon fresh lemon juice

$^1/_2$ cup extra virgin olive oil

$^1/_2$ cup grapeseed or vegetable oil

Place the garlic and salt in a mortar and mash it to a paste. (Alternatively, put the garlic and salt on a cutting board and mash it using the tip and side of a wide chef's knife. Press the garlic against the board, pushing down with the knife to smash the garlic into a paste.)

Put the mashed garlic, egg yolk, and lemon juice in a bowl and whisk to combine. Whisk in the olive oil and grapeseed oil in a slow, thin stream. Whisk continuously until the oil is completely blended in. Cover with plastic wrap and refrigerate for up to 1 week.

Brown Chicken Stock

YIELD: APPROXIMATELY 8 CUPS

6 pounds chicken backs or wings

2 yellow onions, coarsely chopped

2 carrots, peeled and chopped

1 stalk celery, chopped

1 cup dry white wine

12 cups cold water

3 ripe plum tomatoes, chopped

4 cloves garlic, smashed

3 sprigs parsley

2 sprigs thyme

1 bay leaf

4 black peppercorns

Preheat the oven to 450°.

Heat a large roasting pan in the oven until hot. Add the chicken and bake for 30 minutes, until dark brown. Tilt the pan and discard all but 2 tablespoons of the oil that collects in the corner. Add the onions, carrots, and celery to the pan and stir to coat with the oil. Bake for 10 minutes.

Transfer the chicken and vegetables to a large stockpot. Add the wine to the roasting pan and cook for 2 to 3 minutes, scraping the bottom and sides of the pan. Add to the stockpot. Cover with the water and bring to a boil over high heat. Remove any impurities that rise to the surface. Add the tomatoes, garlic, parsley, thyme, bay leaf, and peppercorns. Return to a boil. Decrease the heat to low and cook uncovered on a low simmer for 4 to 6 hours, until the flavor is completely extracted from the chicken and vegetables. Pour through a fine-mesh strainer into a large bowl set in an ice water bath. Transfer to small airtight containers and refrigerate for up to 3 days or freeze for up to 2 months.

Candied Walnuts

YIELD: APPROXIMATELY 3 CUPS

1/4 cup water

1/4 cup honey

1/4 cup sugar

1 pound walnut pieces

Preheat the oven to 400°. Brush a baking sheet with vegetable oil or butter.

Bring the water, honey, and sugar to a boil over high heat. Add the walnuts and cook for 5 minutes, until the nuts are coated and the liquid has evaporated. Spread the nuts out on the baking sheet. Bake for 12 to 15 minutes, stirring occasionally, until evenly browned. Transfer to a clean baking sheet and refrigerate until cool. As soon as they are cool, break the nuts apart with your hands. The candied nuts can be frozen for up to 1 month in an airtight container.

Charmoula

YIELD: 1/2 CUP

1 tablespoon toasted cumin seeds

1 tablespoon toasted coriander seeds

2 tablespoons sweet paprika

1 teaspoon freshly ground black pepper

1/2 teaspoon kosher salt

1/4 teaspoon cayenne pepper

3 cloves garlic, mashed

2 tablespoons water

1 tablespoon fresh lemon juice

1/4 cup extra virgin olive oil

Grind the cumin and coriander together with a mortar and pestle or in a spice grinder. Transfer to a small bowl and add the paprika, black pepper, salt, and cayenne. Stir to combine. Add the garlic and stir, mashing with the back of a wooden spoon until a paste is formed. Add the water and lemon juice; stir until a thick, smooth paste forms. Add the olive oil and stir until incorporated.

Chicken Stock

YIELD: APPROXIMATELY 8 CUPS

6 pounds chicken backs or wings

12 cups cold water

2 yellow onions, coarsely chopped

2 carrots, peeled and chopped

1 stalk celery, chopped

4 cloves garlic, smashed

3 sprigs parsley

2 sprigs thyme

1 bay leaf

4 black peppercorns

Place the chicken in a large stockpot. Cover with the water and bring to a boil over high heat. Remove any impurities that rise to the surface. Add the onions, carrots, celery, garlic, parsley, thyme, bay leaf, and peppercorns. Return to a boil. Decrease the heat and cook uncovered for 4 to 6 hours, until the flavor is completely extracted from the chicken and vegetables. Pour through a fine-mesh strainer into a large bowl set in an ice water bath. Transfer to small airtight containers and refrigerate for up to 3 days or freeze for up to 2 months.

Chipotle-Lime Butter

YIELD: APPROXIMATELY 1 CUP

$1/4$ cup ($1/2$ stick) unsalted butter, cut into cubes, at room temperature

1 chipotle chile in adobo sauce, seeded and finely minced

2 teaspoons adobo sauce

1 teaspoon fresh lime juice

$1/2$ teaspoon minced lime zest

$1/2$ teaspoon kosher salt

Combine the butter, chipotle, adobo sauce, lime juice, lime zest, and salt in a small bowl. Stir with a wooden spoon until smooth. Cover and refrigerate for up to 1 week.

Gremolata

YIELD: APPROXIMATELY 2 TABLESPOONS

2 tablespoons chopped flat-leaf parsley

1 teaspoon chopped garlic

1 teaspoon chopped lemon zest

Combine the parsley, garlic, and lemon zest on a cutting board and chop together into a fine mince. Use immediately.

Harissa

YIELD: 3/4 CUP

4 guajillo or New Mexico chiles

4 tablespoons extra virgin olive oil

2 cloves garlic, minced

3 large ripe plum tomatoes, peeled, seeded, and diced

2 teaspoons fresh lemon juice

1/2 teaspoon ground cumin

Kosher salt

Put the chiles in a small bowl and cover with water. Soak for about 20 minutes, until soft.

Combine 2 tablespoons of the olive oil and the garlic in a large skillet over medium heat for 1 minute. Add the tomatoes and cook for about 10 minutes, or until soft and the moisture is cooked out completely (the oil will begin to separate from the tomatoes). Remove from the heat.

Drain the chiles and squeeze between your hands to remove any excess liquid. Place them in a food processor, add the tomato mixture, and purée. Add the remaining 2 tablespoons olive oil, the lemon juice, cumin, and a pinch of salt. Press with a rubber spatula through a fine-mesh sieve into a bowl. Discard any solids. Transfer to an airtight container and refrigerate until ready to use, for up to 1 month.

Pizza Dough

YIELD: 6 (8-INCH) ROUNDS

2 1/2 cups all-purpose flour

2 cups durum flour

1 tablespoon extra virgin olive oil

1 tablespoon dry active yeast

2 teaspoons kosher salt

1 3/4 cups warm (75°) water

Mix the all-purpose flour, durum flour, olive oil, yeast, and salt together in the bowl of an electric mixer fitted with the dough hook attachment. Add the water. Mix for 2 to 3 minutes, until the dough begins to stick together and form a ball. Transfer to a lightly floured surface and knead the dough for 5 minutes, until smooth and elastic. Place in a lightly oiled bowl and cover with plastic wrap. Set in a warm area for 1 hour, until the dough has doubled in volume. Punch it down to remove the air and divide into 6 equal portions. Roll into 6 balls and set the balls on a floured baking sheet. Cover with plastic wrap and refrigerate for up to 3 hours, until ready to use.

To grill the pizza dough instead of baking in a wood-burning oven: Preheat a gas or charcoal grill to high heat (at least 500°).

Shape each ball into an 8-inch round by stretching or pressing the dough on a lightly floured surface. Brush one side with olive oil and set on the hottest part of the grill, oil side down. Brush the top with olive oil. Cook for 1 minute. Turn at a 90-degree angle and cook for 1 minute. Turn over and repeat on the other side. Add the pizza toppings and cook over indirect heat for 3 to 5 minutes, until the cheese melts.

Richard's Cherry-Cola Barbecue Sauce

YIELD: 3 CUPS

2 tablespoons extra virgin olive oil

1 large yellow onion, minced

3 cloves garlic, minced

8 cups (about 2 liters) cherry cola

2 cups ketchup

1 cup apple cider vinegar

1 tablespoon chopped chipotle chile

2 teaspoons sweet paprika

2 teaspoons freshly ground black pepper

1 teaspoon kosher salt

Heat the olive oil in a large skillet over medium heat. Add the onion and cook for 10 minutes. Add the garlic and cook for 1 to 2 minutes, until soft and golden. Add the cola and bring to a boil. Cook for 45 minutes, until reduced to one-quarter of the amount. Stir in the ketchup, vinegar, chipotle, paprika, pepper, and salt. Cook for 15 minutes, until thick. Refrigerate in an airtight container for up to 1 month.

Roasted Garlic Purée

YIELD: APPROXIMATELY 1 CUP

2 to 3 bulbs garlic

1/4 cup plus 2 tablespoons extra virgin olive oil

Kosher salt

Freshly ground black pepper

1 sprig thyme

Preheat the oven to 400°.

Make a horizontal cut across the top of each bulb of garlic to expose the cloves. Place the bulbs cut side up on a piece of aluminum foil. Pour the 2 tablespoons olive oil over the top and sprinkle with the salt and pepper. Place the thyme on top, seal the foil, and put on a baking sheet. Bake for 1 hour to 1 hour and 15 minutes, until tender. Let cool.

Squeeze the garlic out of the peel into a bowl and mash it with the back of a spoon. Stir in the 1/4 cup olive oil until a smooth paste forms. Cover and refrigerate for up to 48 hours.

Toasted Pumpkin Seeds

YIELD: 1 CUP

2 tablespoons extra virgin olive oil

1 cup pumpkin seeds

1 teaspoon kosher salt

Heat the olive oil in a large nonstick skillet over high heat. Add the pumpkin seeds and cook for about 5 minutes, until lightly browned and the seeds begin to pop, stirring constantly. Transfer to a paper towel–lined plate using a slotted spoon, and sprinkle with the salt. Store in an airtight container for up to 1 week.

TECHNIQUES

Making the Right Size Cuts

Julienne: About 1 inch long and $1/8$-inch thick and wide

Fine dice: $1/8$-inch square or smaller

Dice: $1/4$-inch square

Chopped: $1/2$ inch or larger

Preparing Bread Crumbs

For dry bread crumbs: Cut day-old bread into 2-inch cubes and spread on a baking sheet. Bake at 200° for several hours, until dry, or overnight with just the pilot light on. Crush in a food processor. Store in an airtight container for up to 1 week.

For fresh bread crumbs: Tear stale bread into small pieces and chop in a food processor until fine crumbs are achieved. Store in an airtight container for up to 1 week.

Preparing Fish Fillets

Begin by removing the skin with a very sharp knife. Remove any bones with tweezers or a knife. Trim the sides to remove any thin edges and to form a uniformly thick piece.

Cleaning Leeks

Cut the leeks in half lengthwise and, if only whites are to be used, discard the greens or save them for another use. Cut the whites into the shape and size directed and then place in a small bowl. Cover with cold water and let sit for 20 minutes. Any sand or dirt in the leeks should sink to the bottom. Scoop the leeks out of the bowl, being careful not to disturb any sand or dirt in the bottom of the bowl. Check to be sure there isn't any remaining sand or dirt.

Roasting Peppers

Grill method: Heat a gas or charcoal grill to high heat and set the peppers on the grill over direct heat. Cook for 20 minutes, until charred evenly on all sides, turning about every 5 minutes.

Stove-top or broiler method: Set the peppers directly over a gas flame on top of the stove or under the broiler set on high and cook for 20 minutes, until charred evenly on all sides, turning about every 5 minutes.

Toasting Nuts

Spread the nuts out on a baking sheet and bake at 300° for 5 to 10 minutes for thin-skinned or skinless nuts, such as pecans and pine nuts, and 10 to 15 minutes for thick-skinned nuts, such as hazelnuts. The nuts release their aromas when they are finished.

TOASTING AND GRINDING SEEDS

Put the seeds in a dry small sauté pan. Spread them out into a thin layer and heat over medium heat for 3 to 5 minutes, depending on the type of seed, until they release their aromas or begin to turn brown. Stir frequently to prevent burning. Transfer to a bowl immediately to stop the cooking process. When cool, crush in a spice grinder or in a mortar with a pestle.

PEELING AND SEEDING TOMATOES

Bring a large saucepan of salted water to a boil over high heat. Cut a small X in the bottom of each tomato without cutting into the flesh. Add to the water and cook for 15 to 30 seconds, until the skin begins to pull away from the X. Transfer to a bowl of ice water with a slotted spoon. Peel away the skin, cut the tomato in half horizontally, and push the seeds out with your fingers or thumb. Chop the tomato into the size specified.

BOILING EGGS

Place the eggs in a small saucepan and cover with cold water. Add a generous pinch of salt and bring to a boil over high heat. Reduce the heat to medium-high and cook at a rapid boil for 12 minutes. Immediately place under the tap and run cold water into the pan until the temperature is cool. Repeat until the eggs are cool. Let sit in the water at room temperature for up to 4 hours until ready to peel.

Wine Tasting Glossary

Tasting wine is like appreciating any other type of art. It's subjective, and what each taster likes best is strictly a matter of personal preference. Describing a wine, however, often relies on colloquial terms to express a taster's sensory evaluation of a wine. Typically, evaluating a wine follows a certain regimen. We've provided a brief description of each component and some of the terms used most often to describe each.

COLOR

This is fairly straightforward. Color is evaluated by holding a glass against a white background. Every varietal has a color range, which does not necessarily have any effect on the taste but can sometimes indicate whether the wine is young or older, respectively displaying deep red-purple hues or tints of brown.

AROMA

The perfume of a wine is often telling about the flavors that will appear in the taste, but they aren't always the same. Smelling a wine is also used to detect wines that have spoiled from age, improper storage, or tainted corks. Wines that smell like wet cardboard or a barnyard, or are simply lacking in any fresh fruit aromas, may be indicative of their taste. Sometimes these aromas will blow off, or go away, after the wine sits in the glass for a few minutes, absorbing oxygen.

TASTE

Taste, although almost entirely controlled by smell, is the all-important indicator of whether or not you like a wine. The first question anyone evaluating wine should ask is, "Do I like it?" The answer should serve as the taster's guide.

The taste of a wine can range from extremely pleasant to terrible, depending on several factors—everything from the weather pattern during the growing season to the size of the barrel it was aged in and, of course, the winemaker's skills.

TEXTURE

The fourth part of wine tasting is evaluating the texture of a wine. Sometimes called the mouthfeel, the texture can be one of two things. The first is the perceived weight, or intensity, of a wine. The second is a feeling often effected by the taste. For example, a wine that has strong tannins might feel rough in your mouth. By contrast, a wine with buttery flavors may be perceived as creamy.

COMMON TERMS USED TO DESCRIBE WINES

Acidity: Usually perceived as a tang, a zippiness, or a little zing. Without acid a wine will taste bland and flat.

Body: The body is usually described as light, medium, or heavy, which represents the perception of the wine's weight in your mouth.

Bright: Wines that have a high-acid profile are sometimes described as bright, in the way that a raspberry will taste bright and a banana will taste rich.

Complex: Complexity in a wine represents that there are layers of flavors that the wine may show, reflecting the vineyard, the vintage, the winemaking, and the aging process. These different flavors are usually revealed gradually and can change between when the wine enters your mouth and is swallowed.

Concentration: This could also be described as flavor density and intensity. Think of adding a teaspoon of water to a teaspoon of sugar and then adding a table-spoon of water to a teaspoon of sugar. They both will be sweet, but the former will be more sweet in the same way that a wine with concentrated flavors will be more powerful.

Crisp: This is used to describe wines with a prominent acid profile and wines that feel lively and energetic in your mouth.

Depth: Like concentration, depth indicates that there are layers of flavor in the wine.

Dry: Wines are either sweet or dry depending on whether or not they have residual sugar. Dry wines are those without residual sugar.

Finish: This is the lasting impression a wine leaves in your mouth. Some wines don't have a finish while others seem to linger forever.

Flavor Compounds: These are the flavors detected in the aroma and taste of the wine. They are not added to the wine but are natural compounds in the wine that mani-fest themselves in a wide range of descriptors. They include all of the fruit flavors listed above, as well as vanilla, mocha, cocoa, licorice, cola, cedar, and spices, such as allspice, cloves, pepper, and nutmeg.

Often flavors and aromas will be mentioned as hints, nuances, notes, and essences, which can indicate that the characteristics they describe are present in the wine but are very subtle.

Floral: Many wines will express floral aromas and flavors. Sometimes they are specific, such as rose, geranium, or gardenia, other times the reference is more general.

Fruity/Fruit-Forward: When fruity or fruit-forward is emphasized it typically indicates that the grapes were picked at the peak of maturity and that the flavors of the fruit are very prominent. Every varietal has its own set of fruit flavor descriptors; these include grapefruit, citrus, papaya, melon, pear, lemon, green apple, straw-berry, cherry, berry, plum, cassis, blackberry, and rasp-berry. Sometimes fruit flavors will be characterized more generally, like red fruit, dark fruit, or black fruit.

Mouthfeel: The mouthfeel of a wine is the impression that tannins or acid will make. It can also be affected by how a wine is fermented and aged. Descriptions include smooth, silky, velvety, luscious, creamy, rich, and round.

Oak: Oak flavors are imparted to wine in the winemak-ing and aging processes. They can lend a wide range of flavors, including toasted bread, caramel, butterscotch, toasty oak, and toasty vanilla.

Structure: Structure is usually used in reference to the tannins. It can describe whether or not the tannins are balanced and blend into the overall flavor of the wine, in which case a wine is usually described as having good structure, well-integrated tannins, and even elegant.

Other commonly used terms that are less concrete, such as good, nice, or fresh, are used to emphasize the characteristic they describe, like nice richness or fresh fruit flavors.

Finally, tasting wine is a constantly surprising endeavor. Wine is an organic substance that changes throughout its lifetime, whether it's over a long period of time while it ages in a cellar or during a brief period after being poured into a glass. We hope that you will enjoy our wines at every stage that you taste them. Cheers!

List of Purveyors

Bellwether Farms
9999 Valley Ford Road
Petaluma, CA 94952-9781
Telephone: (707) 763-0993
Website: www.bellwethercheese.com
**The Callahan family produces out-
standing artisan aged sheep's and
cow's milk cheeses.**

Broken Arrow Ranch
P.O. Box 530
Ingram, TX 78025
Telephone: (800) 962-4263
Website: www.brokenarrowranch.com
**Owner, Mike Hughes, raises free-
range wild game such as venison and
antelope.**

The California Press
P.O. Box 408
Rutherford, CA 94573
Telephone: (707) 963-7571
Fax: (707) 944-0350
Website: www.californiapress.com
**Local producer of specialty nut oils
and flours.**

California Vegetable Specialties, Inc.
15 Poppy House Road
Rio Vista, CA 94571
Telephone: (707) 374-2111
Website: www.endive.com
**Year-round grower of California
white and red endive.**

Forni-Brown-Welsh
P.O. Box 3434
900 Foothill Road
Calistoga, CA 94515
Telephone: (707) 942-6123
Fax: (707) 942-8122
**Premier grower of organic lettuces,
greens, herbs, and other garden
delicacies.**

Gerhard's Napa Valley Sausage
910 Enterprise Way
Napa, CA 94558
Telephone: (707) 252-4116
**Producer of fresh, natural, and
healthful gourmet sausages.**

Gourmet Mushrooms
P.O. Box 391
Sebastopol, CA 95472
Telephone: (707) 823-1743
Website:
    www.gourmetmushroomsinc.com
**Cultivators and purveyors of both
common and wild mushrooms. Also
supplies mushrooms for medicinal
purposes.**

Hog Island Oyster Co.
P.O. Box 829
Marshall, CA 94940
Telephone: (415) 663-9218
Website: www.hogislandoyster.com
**Purveyor of organically raised
oysters and clams. Located on the
northern coast of California.**

Laura Chenel's Chevre
4310 Fremont Drive
Sonoma, CA 95476
Telephone: (707) 996-4477
Fax: (707) 996-1816
**Producer of artisan goat's milk
cheeses; founded in 1979.**

Lundberg Rice
P.O. Box 269
Richvale, CA 95974-0369
Telephone: (530) 882-4551
Fax: (530) 882-4500
Website: www.lundberg.com
**Family-owned business growing
organic grains to produce short-
and long-grain specialty rice.**

Marshall's Farm Honey
15 Lombard Road
American Canyon, CA 94503
Telephone: (707) 556-8088
Fax: (707) 556-8083
Website: www.marshallshoney.com
**Gourmet producers of honey from
Northern California bees.**

Napa Valley College Potters Guild
2277 Napa-Vallejo Highway
Napa, CA 94558
Telephone: (707) 253-3205
Website: www.plasm.com/ceramics
**Local potters creating beautiful
ceramic plates, platters, and bowls.**

Napa Valley Lamb Company
4320 B. Old Toll Road
Calistoga, CA 94515
Telephone: (707) 942-6957
Fax: (707) 942-8852
Small family-owned business that produces sustainable-grown lambs.

Omega 3 Seafoods, Inc.
P.O. Box 2692
Napa, CA 94558-0269
Telephone: (707) 252-7674
Local fishmonger supplying fresh seafood and producing house-smoked salmon products.

Point Reyes Farmstead
Cheese Company
P.O. Box 9
Point Reyes Station, CA 94956
Telephone: (415) 663-8880 or
(800) 591-6878
Website: www.pointreyescheese.com
Producers of artisanal-made blue cheeses.

Scharffen Berger Chocolate Maker
914 Heinz Avenue
Berkeley, CA 94710
Telephone: (510) 981-4058 or
(800) 930-4528 (retail orders)
Fax: (510) 981-4051
Website: www.scharffenberger.com
Gourmet producer of delicious dark chocolate.

Skyhill Napa Valley Farms
34 Valley Club Circle
Napa, CA 94558
Telephone: (707) 255-4800
Fax: (707) 252-9297
Email: skyhillfarm@aol.com
Small local purveyor of fresh goat's milk cheese.

Sonoma County Poultry
P.O. Box 140
Penngrove, CA 94951
Telephone: (707) 795-3797 or
(800) 95-DUCKS
Website: www.libertyducks.com
Specialty grower of ducks.

Sparrow Lane Vinegars
1445 Summit Lake Drive
Angwin, CA 94508
Telephone: (707) 965-9130
Fax: (707) 965-9131
Small family-owned business producing wine varietal vinegars.

Timber Crest Farms
4791 Dry Creek Road
Healdsburg, CA 95448
Telephone: (707) 433-8251 or
(888) 374-9325
Fax: (707) 433-8255
Website: www.timbercrest.com
Family-owned business producing organic and preservative-free dried fruits, nuts, and vegetables.

Tomales Bay Foods/Cowgirl
Creamery
P.O. Box 594
Point Reyes Station, CA 94956
Telephone: (415) 663-9335
Fax: (415) 663-5418
Website: www.cowgirlcreamery.com
Purveyor and producer of artisan and farmstead cheeses.

Vella Cheese
315 Second Street East
Sonoma, CA 95476
Telephone: (800) 848-0505
Producer of gourmet aged jack and Cheddar cheeses.

INDEX

✦